In good company

A snapshot of theatre and the Arts

To
Miriam,
With love, and
many, many
thanks!
Nicola
x

Cambridge Arts
Theatre

Previous page:
Cambridge Arts Theatre Open Day.

Opposite:
English Touring Opera in rehearsal
for *The Magic Flute*.

In good company

A snapshot of theatre and the Arts

Photographs by Julia Hedgecoe
Text by Nicola Upson and Mandy Morton
with a foreword by Sir Donald Sinden

First published in Great Britain by Cambridge Arts Theatre, 2005

Cambridge Arts Theatre
6 St. Edward's Passage
Cambridge CB2 3PJ

www.cambridgeartstheatre.com

Supported by TTP Com Limited
www.ttpcom.com

ISBN 0-9547804-0-X

Picture Acknowledgements
The publishers would like to thank the following for their
permission to reproduce additional photographs:
The Cambridgeshire Collection, Cambridge Central Library,
pp 4, 5, 8, 10, 12 (left), 17 (top); Dr M Keynes, pp 1, 3, 13.

Designed by
John Carrod
Carrods@dial.pipex.com
Cambridge

Specialist scanning by
Swaingrove Colourscript
Rougham, Suffolk

Printed in Great Britain by
Piggott Black Bear
Cambridge

TTPCom Limited

TTPCom Limited is the principal operating subsidiary of TTP Communications plc (LSE: TTC). The company develops intellectual property used in the design and manufacture of wireless communication terminals. TTPCom licenses its technology to leading semiconductor and terminal manufacturers worldwide, including Analog Devices, Intel, LG, Renesas, Sharp, Siemens and Toshiba.

TTPCom has established an industry standard with its GPRS platform, offers EDGE, 3G, Wireless LAN and Wireless PAN solutions and, for those manufacturers for whom a fast time to market is critical, TTPCom also offers complete handset and module designs. Over 23 million devices using TTPCom technology were shipped globally during 2003. More information can be found on TTPCom's website at: http://www.ttpcom.com.

The policy TTPCom Limited has adopted concerning charitable donations is one of support within the area for theatres, schools, hospitals, music, and local communities. We enthusiastically support personal endeavours that are relevant to employees of the company and attempt to match sponsorship raised by participants in various sporting and fundraising events, as well as endorsing personal requests for donations to organisations which are thought to be relevant to our criteria.

We are delighted to be the sponsor of In Good Company.

Many colourful personalities have graced the

Arts Theatre's stage but, behind the scenes, one of

the most gregarious and inspirational figures was

Andrew Blackwood, whose good company saw the

Theatre safely through thirty-two years.

This book is dedicated to his tremendous achievement,

 with thanks and many happy memories.

Contents

Foreword

I feel very privileged to have spent a great deal of my working life in beautiful theatres around the country. Touring is a wonderful thing: not only does it provide endless opportunities for an ecclesiologist and inveterate sightseer like myself, but it bonds actors together as great friends and has allowed me to form so many lasting links all over Britain. Nowhere holds any terrors for me, but Cambridge is a particular joy. I have played the Arts Theatre twice since its refurbishment, once in Ronald Harwood's *Quartet* and most recently in *The Hollow Crown*, which was devised and directed by John Barton, my guru and himself a great Cambridge man. It is a marvellous stage to perform on for an actor, and the auditorium holds a very special place for me, too: there, in the stalls, are two seats given by Sir Geoffrey Cass and named in memory of my beloved son, Jeremy, who spent a period of time on the stage crew at the Arts Theatre before going on to be a splendid actor.

Theatre is an ephemeral thing: no two performances are identical, and that is its magic. Because I also work in television, people often ask me which I prefer, but there really is no question: if your game is football and you are offered two tickets for the cup final or the chance to watch it on television, you will always choose to be there – and theatre is the same; it happens now, this minute. Theatre-going is a habit, and that is what we have to encourage because audience contact is central to every performance. It is our job as actors to cajole an audience, to win it over, to take an auditorium full of disparate people – all of whom have had strange, disparate days – and to make them behave as a single body. For that to work, the audience has to give as much as the actors.

The most wonderful person to have in an audience was Dame Sybil Thorndike. She loved the theatre and would always sit in the front row, leaning forward from the moment the house-lights went down, ready to enjoy what was to come; she was the first to laugh, her eyes forever darting left and right, and she never missed a trick. A friend of mine once went to see a play at the Royal Court. Five minutes before curtain-up, a very old couple entered the auditorium and sat in the seats in front of him. They were Sybil Thorndike and her husband, Lewis Casson; Sybil was 85 and Lewis was 92. When the house-lights dimmed, she turned to him and said 'Oh Lewis! I do so love a play, don't you!?' 'I do so love a play' is surely the motto of every theatregoer.

As the Arts Theatre moves further into a new century – one in which theatre faces different challenges every day – I hope its audiences will continue to share that spirit of enthusiasm and excitement which makes every performance memorable and unique.

Donald Sinden

Sir Donald Sinden

Introduction

Maynard Keynes –
inspirational economist and
founder of Cambridge Arts
Theatre – in his library.

The night of 3 February, 1936 was a cold one, but fine – and that, at least, was a blessing for those whose only concern was the readiness of a splendid new building on Cambridge's Peas Hill. As is often the case with such an undertaking, things were running a little behind schedule; many had worked all through the previous night to ensure that the first visitors through the modest front entrance would not be met by wet plaster and draughty doors and, as late as three o'clock in the afternoon, glass was still to be polished and an anxious eye awaited the arrival of the final consignment of French linen, ordered in London and transformed locally into table-cloths and napkins for the restaurant. It was probably just as well that, for the first two days, the doors were open to invited guests only; not until lunchtime on the first public day would the stair-carpets be properly fixed into place and the required licences actually obtained. But as it was nothing less than a miracle of personal conviction that the plans had progressed this far, the loss of a few months seemed a small price to pay; and by this time, no one closely involved was in any doubt that the city's new theatre would be worth the wait, worth the sleepless nights.

Surprisingly enough, when the Arts Theatre opened its doors for the first time, Cambridge was suffering from a distinct lack of theatre and had been for at least three years; the ADC had burnt down in 1933 and was only just getting back on its feet; the New Theatre had been taken over for use as the city's tenth cinema; and the Festival Theatre, internationally renowned during the late 1920s and early 1930s for seasons directed by Terence Gray, Anmer Hall and Norman Marshall, had finally run out of wealthy sponsors. Little wonder, then, that the body of people intent on braving the February cold did so with a kind of festive reverence, characteristic of those attending church on Christmas Eve: made up of local dignitaries and noted critics, of those who had contributed financially or professionally to the building's realisation, of anybody living nearby who might be disturbed by its future activities and needed to be won over from the outset, this select group of a little over six hundred had come to give its verdict on one man's gift to the town. Unusually for a first night, the attention of the audience was divided between the performances on stage and the hitherto-concealed bricks and mortar – and neither let them down. Few would have believed that a spacious and aesthetically-satisfying theatre could be created on such a cramped and ungiving site, hidden behind inadequate entrances; the same astonishment is evident in the faces of

GALA
PERFORMANCES

ON THE OCCASION OF
THE OPENING OF THE

ARTS THEATRE
OF CAMBRIDGE

... ...

MONDAY, 3rd FEBRUARY, 1936, at 8.30

'THE VIC-WELLS BALLET'

... ...

TUESDAY, 4th FEBRUARY, 1936, at 8.30

'MASQUERADE'

I

Lydia Lopokova and Maynard Keynes, 1929. Keynes was a shrewd collector of art: Cézanne's *L'Oncle Dominique* is on the wall.

first-time audiences to this day, because there are still few auditoriums anywhere in the country which can match the elegant simplicity of its décor or the gentle intimacy which it offers to the actors and their audience.

But if a sleight of hand had been performed in the building, nothing less magical was taking place on stage. The redoubtable Lilian Baylis, founder of The Old Vic and Sadler's Wells, had long ago promised that the Vic-Wells Ballet would give the gala performance for the opening night, beginning a long and mutually-rewarding relationship that brought prestige to Cambridge and gave Baylis access to the University audience in whose hands she believed the future of theatre to sit. Under the direction of Ninette de Valois, the programme for that first evening featured the 'Pas de Trois' from *Swan Lake*,

together with *Les Rendezvous, The Rake's Progress, Siesta* and *Façade;* the orchestra, conducted by Constant Lambert, contributed two interludes by Chabrier and the dancers included Pearl Argyle, June Brae, Pamela May, Frederick Ashton, Robert Helpmann, Michael Somes, Harold Turner and a young ballerina called Margot Fonteyn. It was the first of many distinguished moments of cultural history to find a home at the Arts.

The earliest applause of the night, however, was not for the performers but for the genial-looking man who took his seat in the box to the right of the stage just a few minutes before half past eight. John Maynard Keynes was a Cambridge man through and through, born in the city and resident there for most of his life. He claimed strong connections with both

The auditorium, 1936.

town and gown – his father was Registrary of the University and, in 1932, his mother became Cambridge's first female Mayor – and he was a Fellow of King's College from 1909 until his death in 1946. The founding of the Arts Theatre had, for Keynes, a very personal rationale: it was a fitting expression of his devotion to his birthplace and home; and it offered a rewarding canvas on which to combine his two greatest qualities – a fine artistic imagination and a profound economic knowledge. The idea of establishing a theatre in the city had been in his mind for more than twenty years; in 1913, following a visit to Birmingham's Repertory Theatre, he wrote enthusiastically to his friend and Bloomsbury intimate, Duncan Grant, that 'This is exactly what we ought to have in Cambridge' and, in 1933, he dedicated himself seriously to the task. Possessing by this time a formidable reputation, considerable wealth and a remarkable talent for inspiring others to work until they dropped, he enlisted the help of Shakespearean scholar and King's Fellow George

Rylands, who was also a talented actor and producer, and Norman Higgins, founder of the Cosmopolitan Cinema in Market Passage, the earliest specialist picture house outside London. Higgins was to be the Arts Theatre's first General Manager, with a special responsibility for arranging film programmes during the weeks that suitable stage productions were not available.

Initially, Keynes estimated the cost of the project to be in the region of £20,000, but the inclusion of film and elaborate staging equipment, modern lighting, auditorium furnishings and a restaurant increased the establishment expenses to £35,000. Half of that sum was raised by a mortgage and later paid off, leaving a net balance of £17,500 which was subscribed personally by the founder as the basic capital employed – an investment, by today's standards, of close on a million pounds. A man of his background and expertise was, of course, always mindful of the economics of art but

Jean Forbes Robertson as Hedda Gabler in the 1936 cycle of Ibsen plays, designed by Motley and financed privately by Keynes.

Photograph by Ramsey and Muspratt

George Rylands
on stage in
*The Duchess
of Malfi.*

Rylands with Clive Swift in rehearsal for the 1986 fund-raising gala.

House, Covent Garden in 1933. The exuberance and comedy that had enhanced her dancing, however, were significantly less advantageous to a woman hoping to make a career as a classical actress, and her pronounced Russian accent would frequently defeat any efforts on behalf of the audience to appreciate the sincerity with which she delivered her lines; as Olivia in *Twelfth Night* – alongside Flora Robson and Charles Laughton in Tyrone Guthrie's Old Vic production – she was a disaster, as Woolf had bitchily predicted she would be because she 'speaks English like a parrokeet'. Keynes felt his wife's disappointment keenly: after her *Twelfth Night* humiliation at the hands of the press, he urged 'Don't be too sad about the acting. I swear we will have another go', and, in 1936, with artistic control of his own stage, he was in a position to offer something more effective than positive words to rescue his wife's career and

Keynes had a third reason for creating his own stage, one which was perhaps more personally felt than even his career or his birthplace: in August 1925, he had married the Russian ballerina Lydia Lopokova, much against the advice of a protective Bloomsbury set. Lopokova was a dancer with the Diaghilev Company and the couple had first met at the end of the war in 1918. Keynes' infatuation with her was shared by the rest of London: audiences welcomed her graceful and entrancing performances with ovations which, said *The Times*, 'can surely seldom have been equalled'; a close friend of Picasso, who sketched her often, the romance surrounding Lopokova was only increased by a mysterious two-year disappearance which drove Bloomsbury, and in particular Virginia Woolf and Vanessa Bell, to frenzied heights of curiosity that would never be entirely satisfied. When she reappeared in 1921, it was to an extended season in London which included roles in *The Sleeping Princess*, the title of which – according to Diaghilev – had been changed from *The Sleeping Beauty* because of the ugliness of her nose. The production was not a success, finishing after three months instead of the planned six – months in which Keynes had often sat alone in the stalls. Not long after her marriage, Lopokova began to take more seriously her second love; as a child performer in St. Petersburg, she had taken great pleasure in acting as well as dancing and had turned professionally to the former even before her final appearance as a ballerina at the Royal Opera

THE OBJECTS OF THE THEATRE

... ...

THE object of the Arts Theatre of Cambridge is the entertainment of the University and Town. Its name describes, and the form of a Pentagon given to its auditorium by the architect symbolises, its purpose of providing a home in Cambridge for the five arts of drama, opera, ballet, music and cinema.

No permanent company will be maintained, but the theatre and its organisation will provide opportunities for at least four classes of production.

(i) In the first place, the theatre will be available for dramatic and musical enterprises staged and produced in Cambridge. For example, the Greek Play will be given here at the end of this term ; the Rodney Dramatic Club will occupy the theatre for a week of the vacation ; and early next term the Cambridge University Musical Society will produce the first performance given on any stage of a new comic opera by Ralph Vaughan Williams.

(ii) From time to time the management of the theatre will itself take the responsibility of producing plays. The first of these occasions will be the production in February of a cycle of four plays by Ibsen described below.

(iii) It is hoped that plays from the West End with their London casts will be available from time to time, either immediately before, or immediately after, their appearance in London.

(iv) It is hoped that some of the leading repertory companies of the country and international touring companies will come to Cambridge to give some of the more successful items in their repertory.

On the cinema side the films given will be of the character already associated with the name of our Manager, Mr. Openshaw Higgins ; that is to say, European productions of conspicuous merit will take a more prominent part in the programme than is usual in other picture houses.

On Sunday evenings some concerts and lectures will be arranged for each term.

3

The Arts Theatre was Keynes' gift to Cambridge and to his wife, the Russian ballerina Lydia Lopokova, who starred in the first dramas to be staged there.

PHOTOGRAPHS BY RAMSEY AND MUSPRATT

reputation. He did so to great effect as soon as he could: the first drama to be staged during the Arts Theatre's opening season was a quartet of plays by Ibsen, financed privately by Keynes and starring Lopokova as Nora Helmer in *A Doll's House* and Hilda Wangel in *The Master Builder*. Designed and costumed by the talented trio, Motley, who had come to prominence for their work with Gielgud in the early 1930s, the season also starred Jean Forbes Robertson in *Hedda Gabler* and *Rosmersholm*, and transferred to London's Criterion Theatre; reactions to the productions as a whole were mixed, but even Woolf conceded that Lopokova had been a success and her gratitude to her husband was touchingly understated: 'I am still delighted with the theatre', she wrote to Keynes shortly afterwards. 'It was more than nice of you to do it for me.'

Keynes' optimism regarding his wife's endeavours was typical of his approach to life in general, and certainly stood as the driving force behind the founding of the Arts Theatre. Whilst he and Rylands and Higgins had formidable expertise between them, it was not necessarily in building and running an ambitious venue; Keynes remained undeterred, though, believing in the advantages of starting from scratch, 'unburdened by notions which might prove inappropriate to the present venture'. The architect for the project was another of Keynes' friends, George Kennedy, who had undertaken work at King's College and at Tilton, Keynes' country home in Sussex, and who had also designed the Tavistock Theatre in Tottenham Court Road.

Kennedy was not the most conventional of architects, but this was not the most conventional of commissions: sketches on the back of an envelope would pass from him to the contractors, and would be miraculously transformed into spaces that were both functional and pleasing to the eye, and which defied the almost-insurmountable limitations of the site. The building process was fraught with difficulty: not only did the new building only just fit into the yards of King's College lodging houses facing Peas Hill and St. Edward's Passage, but access to the irregularly-shaped plot was confined to a small entrance passage, the use of which was shared with the residents of a large college lodging house. Even Keynes could not persuade another college to relinquish a few square yards of the Eagle Courtyard, which left the Arts – until its 1996 refurbishment – with a wedge-shaped stage that greatly restricted its potential for ballet and large-scale musicals and opera. Nevertheless, Kennedy

The Footlights May Week Revue, 1937.

remained remarkably relaxed throughout: on one occasion, recalled by Norman Higgins who had become an unofficial Clerk of Works, he travelled up from his Chelsea studio to see a particular piece of brickwork, only to discover that it was not yet ready for his inspection; unperturbed, the architect simply looked at the sky and observed that it was a delightful day for a trip to the country, suggesting that Higgins drove him to Papworth to see what progress had been made on a desk designed for his office and adding that he had a picnic lunch for two; in due course, he produced a bag of raw carrots and another of plums.

But although the actual construction had its inherent nightmares, the creation of the Arts Theatre's interior and soul must have been a joy for all involved, combining as it did the selection of a series of cultural gems with an extensive communal shopping trip. It is not hard to imagine the spirit of excitement in which Higgins and Keynes and their wives visited Liberty and the Galeries Lafayette in

Robert Helpmann, one of many notable Hamlets to have taken to the stage at the Arts.

London to choose 350 hand towels for the lavatories, or the endless trials and discussions that must have taken place before the auditorium seating – installed at 24/3d a seat – was finally decided upon. Some investments proved more enduring than others, of course: the lighting and seating served for more than thirty years; the hand towels mysteriously disappeared within the first three months, together with most of the Theatre's silver-crested cutlery. But all were made with a very clear vision of the building's lasting importance, and Keynes was at the centre of it all, attending to the detail as well as to the greater whole. He made cuts where necessary – the plaster masked motifs which decorated the proscenium arch were going to be proper oak when the money could be spared but the craftsman died before such luxuries could be entertained – but knew where not to stint, and the backstage conditions were a particular priority: influenced by Lopokova's bad experiences as a performer, he was determined that the dressing rooms

should be as comfortable for the actors as the front-of-house facilities were for the audience.

Other aspects of the Arts Theatre's personality were developed with an air of eccentricity that the venue has never entirely shaken off, nor would it wish to do so: the orchestra pit was designed around the 39-piece Sadler's Wells Orchestra, and the required space was painstakingly calculated by asking someone to simulate the playing of each and every instrument while a chalk line was drawn around the occupied area; the Circle, originally made to seat 250 people, was tested for safety on the insistence of Cambridgeshire's Chief Constable by asking 350 undergraduates to spend one Sunday lunchtime jumping up and down in it simultaneously, the risk to their health being compensated for with a liberal supply of sherry; and having declared that not enough Champagne was drunk in Cambridge, Keynes single-handedly set about resolving the problem by insisting on a mark-up of only 2/6d instead of the usual fifty per cent. After the opening, as chairman of the Arts Theatre Company, Keynes remained a dominant force in everything from the selling of the tickets to the production of plays, despite a near-fatal coronary thrombosis in May, 1937.

One of the most difficult tasks proved to be choosing a name which would both suit the Theatre's objectives and appeal to future audiences. Inspired by the fact that, for centuries, fish stalls had filled Peas Hill, Keynes suggested The Fishmarket Theatre but was promptly informed by Rylands that the idea 'stank'; King's, Granta and Cam were all mooted and instantly rejected for being too localised, and eventually the Arts Theatre was chosen by default, simply because it seemed the most innocuous compromise. In its seventy year history, that juxtaposition of two words as capable of causing suspicion as any others in the language has occasionally led to false assumptions of elitism, but the name remains appropriate to a theatre which has consistently nurtured and developed all art forms, from drama and film to dance, opera and orchestral music and, more recently, literature and the visual arts. The pentagonal shape of the auditorium, together with the adoption of a pentagon for its logo, symbolises the Arts' commitment to providing a home in Cambridge for the five arts of drama, opera, ballet, music and cinema.

The American monologist Ruth Draper: after making her English debut at the Cambridge YMCA, she began a love affair with the Arts Theatre during her 1936 sell-out performances there.

As the performance drew to a close on that opening night, and the dancers took the first of seven curtain calls, Keynes left the box where he had been sitting with his wife and the Vice Chancellor of the University and made his way downstairs to deliver his speech. As he appeared on stage, the applause died down and the audience waited patiently for him to speak, less in anticipation of what he had to say than to take their first opportunity of the evening to test the acoustics of the spoken word; from the front of the stalls to the back of the circle, they heard everything perfectly.

At the supper party in the restaurant afterwards, the euphoria and the relief were palpable. There was, of course, a speech of thanks to Keynes, delivered by Provost Sheppard of King's after a perilous climb onto the table at which he was sitting; on his return to floor-level, he, in his

The West End star Flora Robson made several appearances at the Arts Theatre: as an undergraduate in Cambridge, Rylands remembered her as 'a great comic actress'.

Keynes hoped that the Arts Theatre's restaurant would encourage undergraduates to drink wine rather than spirits; vintage Krug was sold for 15s, less than half the price charged at the Savoy.

turn, was congratulated for his athleticism by Lilian Baylis, whose presence at the main table had enlivened the conversation considerably; the evening had been punctuated by her voice – rough and warm and a little Cockney – rising above the less uninhibited tones, and a cheer had spread round the room as she was heard to declare to a rather nervous chaplain from one of the colleges, 'Church and stage – same thing; well, it should be!' with that characteristic twist in the mouth which everyone imitated when repeating one of her priceless remarks. Eventually, it was time for Miss Baylis to shepherd her boys and girls reluctantly onto their coach for the journey back to London; it departed in the early hours, but only after Baylis had made some pungent comments about the

Keynes with
George Bernard
Shaw on the
steps of the
Fitzwilliam
Museum,
Cambridge,
in 1936.

non-appearance of Robert Helpmann and issued instructions that 'the bounder' was to be found in time to be put on the first train in the morning. After the excitement of the stage and the glamour of the first-night party, Higgins returned to the restaurant to discover – if he had not already – that his role as General Manager required him to be everything from stage manager, carpenter, electrician and painter to cook, waiter and wine merchant, accountant, dietician and diplomat; good-humouredly, he calmed the ruffled feathers in the kitchen and immersed himself in the washing up of dishes, crockery, glass and cutlery for a party of sixty.

Trevor Nunn outside the Festival Theatre. The historic building, designed by William Wilkins Jnr, was owned by Cambridge Arts Trust from the 1940s to the 1990s.

The very next evening, they did it all again but this time the gala performance was designed to show off the Theatre's brand new cinema equipment and Higgins – whose specialist field this was – was in his element. The programme began with a Disney cartoon, British Movietone News, and the world premiere of the GPO Film Unit production, *Night Mail*, with music by Benjamin Britten and a commentary written and spoken by WH Auden; the main film was Willie Forst's *Masquerade*, which had recently set a British box office record at the newly-opened Curzon Cinema in Mayfair. The fanfare preceding and following the announcements was specially composed for the Arts Theatre by Walter Leigh, recorded by Decca and played by members of the London Symphony Orchestra.

In Rylands' opinion, the Arts Theatre gave Keynes the happiest ten years of his life outside of his marriage. At his premature death, in April 1946, he was still heavily involved in its activities and, with Britain once again at peace, was looking forward to a future in Cambridge with his books and his art and his friends, finally free of the arduous wartime duties that had taken such a toll on his health. He had been offered and had accepted the Order of Merit, a royal honour reserved for just twenty-four people at any one time, and the future of his theatre looked encouraging, with no hint of the financial crises and dwindling audiences that were to threaten its existence at regular intervals from the 1950s onwards. His control of the Arts may have spanned only ten years out of nearly seventy but his legacy has lasted and, without exception, those who have taken over the reins in subsequent years have shared and developed his vision.

As Rylands eloquently wrote on his death, 'No man in our time has put leisure to finer use or worked harder to enable others to enjoy or use their leisure well.'

By the time the Arts Theatre held another gala opening, sixty years later and in celebration of the major refurbishment which followed a Lottery award, little – and everything – had changed. Once again, there was a new building with much to admire – even if the first audiences through the door did have to share the space with those still working to finish it off. Once again, it had been sensitively designed for those back stage and front-of-house by ex Footlights member Barry Brown, but this time the Theatre boasted improvements to dressing rooms, ventilation and catering facilities, and was able to join its entrances at ground level for the first time; extensive rebuilding – only one original wall in the auditorium remained – allowed issues of access to be successfully addressed; and, at last, a higher fly tower and squaring-off of the restrictive triangular stage enabled the Arts to take the larger-scale shows that it had been wanting to attract for so long. So once again, the Theatre's beautiful auditorium, still with its unusual pentagonal shape, was the building's heart and soul, offering opening seasons that embraced classic drama, dance, opera, modern plays, films and productions staged by town and University societies.

In the intervening years, the Arts Theatre repeatedly lived through financial crises and poor audience figures; its future,

Cambridge Arts Theatre presents the Longborough Festival Opera production of

THE RING

Das Rheingold ◆ Die Walküre ◆ Siegfried ◆ Götterdämmerung

By Richard Wagner

'A STUNNING
ACHIEVEMENT.'
Opera Now

Performed in the acclaimed
shortened version prepared for
Birmingham City Opera by
Jonathan Dove and Graham Vick.

Cambridge Arts
Theatre

8 – 14 July 2002
Box Office: 01223 503333

The 2002 presentation of Longborough Festival Opera's *Ring Cycle* was the first time that Wagner's great work had been seen in Cambridge.

Cambridge Theatre Company, later Method & Madness, was established in 1970 and soon became one of the most highly-respected touring companies in the country; Sheila Hancock, Maureen Lipman, Zoë Wanamaker, Ian Charleson, Prunella Scales and Tom Conti were among those who played seasons with the company.

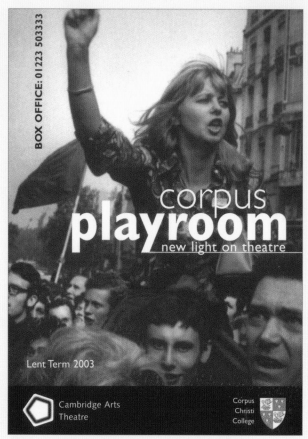

In joining with Corpus Christi College to manage the Playroom, the Arts Theatre has created 'a safe place to be dangerous' for new writers.

wrote the *Cambridge Daily News* back in 1957, 'rests fairly and squarely on the shoulders of the theatre-loving public' and, while its modern fate depends on a more complex and often conflicting group of interested parties, such a statement would not be out of place in today's press. It is remarkable to see how what we regard as twenty-first century concerns – ageing audiences, last-minute booking patterns, even parking provision – go back at least to the 1950s, and perhaps even earlier. But the fact that enough people still cannot imagine life without the Arts is thanks to its dogged determination to look to the future. Since Keynes first established the Arts Theatre's objectives back in 1936, it has always been in its nature to lead and, while those who have inherited his responsibilities have had very different backgrounds and ambitions, they have all had one thing in common: a belief that the greatest tradition is innovation.

Cyril Fletcher and Christopher Biggins: through good story-telling and fine productions, these two famous dames stamped their mark on traditional pantomime, breaking box office records year after year and gaining a loyal Cambridge following.

CAMBRIDGE ARTS THEATRE

FOUNDED IN 1936 BY LORD KEYNES
Licensee and Managing Director   Norman Higgins

Christmas Season
1954

THE CAMBRIDGE ARTS THEATRE
presents

CYRIL FLETCHER
BETTY ASTELL

IN A NEWLY COMMISSIONED
PANTOMIME PRODUCTION

THE QUEEN
OF HEARTS

This production is to be presented from
25 January to 5 February, 1955
at the
FESTIVAL THEATRE, MALVERN

PROGRAMME
SIXPENCE

THE TRUSTEES AND DIRECTORS HOPE ALL PATRONS
WILL ENJOY ATTRACTIVE FARE ON STAGE AND
SCREEN AND IN THE RESTAURANT AND BUFFET BAR
THROUGHOUT 1955.

The Pied Pipers' 1973 production of *Fiddler on the Roof* (directed by Rex Freeman and revived in 2004) and Stephen Siddall's 2003 *Duchess of Malfi*: amateur productions from the town and university form a central and popular part of the Arts Theatre's programme.

More than most provincial theatres, the story of the Arts is the story of the people who have run it and each has stamped his personality on an increasingly rich organisation, from Keynes and Higgins and Rylands to ex-naval Commander Andrew Blackwood, whose dedication steered the Theatre through thirty-two often turbulent years, and his successor, Stephen Walton, who was charged with the unenviable task of overseeing Lottery bids and rebuilding.

All have shown courage, energy and expertise in many different areas and recent years are no exception: under Ian Ross and Nigel Brown as Executive Director and Chairman, the Arts Theatre enjoyed its most exciting period for some time, punching far above its weight – just as it did in its opening years – by attracting artists of the highest calibre and embarking upon such ambitious projects

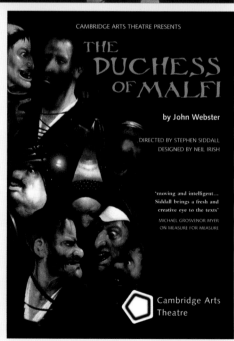

CAMBRIDGE ARTS THEATRE PRESENTS

THE DUCHESS OF MALFI

by John Webster

DIRECTED BY STEPHEN SIDDALL
DESIGNED BY NEIL IRISH

'moving and intelligent...
Siddall brings a fresh and
creative eye to the texts'
MICHAEL GROSVENOR MYER
ON MEASURE FOR MEASURE

Cambridge Arts Theatre

The Arts Theatre's award-winning education programme includes open days, dance projects, BSL interpreted performances, schools matinees and pantomime workshops for the elderly frail, and embraces the whole community.

as Cambridge's first presentation of Wagner's *Ring Cycle*. In the six years of Ross' tenure, the Arts was never afraid to be a theatre of contradiction: to build a national significance whilst remaining true to its local roots; to plan for the future whilst honouring a unique past; and to blur outmoded distinctions between the innovative and the commercial in favour of a diversity that today's audience actually wants.

Thanks to Ross' belief in the possibilities of a theatre grounded in realistic economy, the first years of the twenty-first century have seen the Arts revive and develop some of the twentieth's most popular conventions. Between 1949 and 1972, Cyril Fletcher – one of Britain's best-known comedians – was responsible for almost twenty Cambridge pantomimes; a household name who, before the war, was popular enough to have four or five separate cabaret bookings in a single night, Fletcher established a successful style of Christmas show which relied on familiar jokes, set routines and a wonderful rapport between the actors on stage and the children in the audience. The pantomimes were written and produced by Fletcher's wife, Betty Astell, and often featured their daughter, Jill; at the centre of them all, though, was his memorable performance as Dame, complete with rosy nose and cheeks, ungainly bulk and high-pitched, cheeky voice. The model of the in-house Christmas production which Fletcher developed was revived in 1999, when Christopher Biggins began a five-year run of directing and starring in the Theatre's annual panto; rooted firmly in the traditions of good storytelling and fine performances, Biggins' shows – like Fletcher's before him – offered quality and continuity instead of soap-star appearances and novelty value, providing good all-round family entertainment and breaking box office records year after year.

The Arts Theatre's commitment to staging – and in some cases funding – local amateur shows remains as strong as it ever was. Trust productions, as they are called, go back to a decision made by Keynes and Higgins in 1938 that the Theatre would take responsibility for 'approved productions of University and Town organisations', and they form a mutually beneficent arrangement unique to Cambridge: the productions staged here each year by, amongst others, Rex Freeman and the Pied Pipers, Stephen Siddall's company and the Cambridge Operatic Society have proved to be some of the most warmly-received; and, through organisations such as the Greek and Marlowe

Societies, national stage, film and television continue to reap the rewards of an arrangement which gives talented young actors, directors and designers their first opportunity to work in a professional theatre with the full co-operation and inspiration of professional staff at all levels. In recent years, the relationship between Cambridge Arts Theatre and student drama has been taken a stage further as the Arts has joined forces with Corpus Christi College to manage the Playroom, a unique L-shaped studio theatre nearby which is famously associated with *avant garde* drama, particularly new writing.

Few things which fall under the banner of a theatre's work have changed more than its definition of the word 'education': in the Arts Theatre's near seventy-year history, its commitment to the principle has always been strong – again, that ever-watchful eye on the future – but has grown from a simple provision of preferential rates and matinee performances for school parties into a multi-layered, award-winning resource that embraces its community at all possible points of connection. The Education and Community Department, under the imaginative leadership of Roberta Hamond, now has a vast and varied remit that covers anything from taking Shakespeare into schools to running an elderly frail panto workshop; from devising a ground-breaking integrated deaf and hearing summer school to providing audio described brochures; and from managing an experimental studio space to being the first point of contact for customers with special needs. But the common denominator in all its activities is the firm belief that being moved by the power of live performance is an experience that enriches and empowers people's lives and that, as such, it should be open to everyone.

The Arts is fortunate always to have held a special place in the hearts of performers: the popular American monologist Ruth Draper declared after her first visit that she had fallen in love with the Theatre and wished she could transport it to wherever she was performing; John Gielgud, Peggy Ashcroft, Sybil Thorndike, Flora Robson, Derek Jacobi, Ian McKellen, Trevor Nunn, Donald Sinden and Peter Hall are among the many to have paid tribute to the special intimacy between stage and auditorium; and Pete Postlethwaite recently startled the members of Gone to Lunch, the Theatre's club for those over 55, by daring to ask: 'Do you know how lucky you are to have this theatre?'. Writers, too, have appreciated its spirit of adventure: during one of the many appeals to

The Arts Theatre's auditorium as it is today, still with a pentagonal shape and a special intimacy between actors and their audience.

safeguard its future, letters flooded in from all over England recalling with gratitude happy evenings spent in the Theatre; among the first to make donations were Agatha Christie and EM Forster, who presented the royalties from the successful stage adaptation of *A Passage to India*.

Theatre is hard work, for all involved. *In Good Company* is at once a tribute to those who, as managers, have brought the Arts this far and to those who continue to sustain its very core with their performances, direction and choreography. Most of this book's contributors, as they will tell you in their own words, juggle the demands of different media including film, television and radio; almost without exception, though, they return to the theatre again and again as the benchmark for all that they do and as the most rewarding experience of

their careers. What follows, as the title suggests, is not in any way a comprehensive history of the stage or of any one life, but a fascinating insight into theatre in general, and the Arts Theatre in particular.

Opposite:
English Touring Opera in rehearsal
for *The Magic Flute*.

In good company

Nigel Brown

Chairman

My first visit to the Arts was, I believe, in 1961. It was a school trip to see the Greek Play, which was the *Antigone* of Sophocles. I remember that the production was heavily criticised because the Chorus was dressed in Minoan loin cloths. The make-up was also very Cretan, I recall! I'm glad that we still do the Greek Play and that the Marlowe is a frequent visitor: maintaining a connection with the University is important given the Theatre's origins, even though we now have to play to a much wider audience.

I have very much enjoyed my involvement with the Arts Theatre. I grew up just down the road from the Shakespeare Memorial Theatre at Stratford and I saw many, many great productions whilst I was at school – very many of them directed or acted in by Cambridge alumni who had cut their theatrical teeth here. Occasionally, things I saw and loved at Stratford all those years ago have reappeared here, such as *Brief Lives* and *The Hollow Crown*. And then there has been my panto education; I suppose beginning with Biggins is about as good as it gets!

As everyone knows, the play's the thing, but not without the theatre and the staff that make it happen. During the long rebuilding period, the memory of the Arts faded so much within the community that the last eight years have had to take the form of a very patient renaissance. The theatre now stands poised for the next phase of its by no means uncolourful history, but it will continue to need considerable amounts of goodwill, determination, ingenuity and, of course, some money over and above what it can earn. Luckily there are local and national funders who appreciate what has been achieved and therefore stand ready and able to help, for which we should all be very grateful.

The Theatre's Board and its staff relish the challenge of making our voice heard above the noise of competing entertainments, most of which have much greater resources and apparent glamour. But the conviction remains that the play's the thing, and it's right, too. This book shows why.

Dave Murphy

Executive Director, 2004 –

I'm excited and honoured to be leading such a wonderful and historic theatre. The Arts is a much-loved Cambridge institution, one which has enjoyed considerable theatrical success since its reopening in 1996, and it is my intention to build on an outstanding reputation for the future.

Most of my education and professional training has been in overwhelmingly rational and quantitative fields. Theatre and opera have always provided me with a means of breaking through the barriers erected by excessive logic; of seeing the world through different and often more compassionate eyes. I remember many years ago reading a book called *The Art of Possibility* by the conductor Benjamin Zander and being struck by his notion that 'Art is about rearranging us, creating surprising juxtapositions, emotional openings, startling presences, flight paths to the eternal'; that is a perfect summary of why I love the theatre. Live performance has always captivated me because of its unpredictability, the interaction with the audience and the fact that, for the length of the piece, nothing else matters.

I have been coming to the Arts Theatre regularly since the early 1990s and have always been amazed by the quality and diversity of what was on my doorstep. Even then, the auditorium was almost womb-like in its intimacy: I felt that all the actors were talking to me and that I was a critical part of the play. Once I joined the Board and became increasingly involved, I was irretrievably hooked. One of the defining moments for me was seeing Shared Experience's production of *Gone to Earth*. The show blended theatre, dance and music, and resonated with me on a number of levels. At the time I was facing some difficult choices in my own life and the play helped me to decide that, however my career developed, I wanted to try to work in the performing arts field. It fundamentally shifted my thinking and opened up new possibilities for me. It was in short all that I regard as the best in theatre.

The trouble with the really magical moments in the arts is that – by their very nature – they cannot be explained: what is it that raises the hairs on the back of your neck or sends shivers down your spine? I was truly humbled by our recent integrated deaf and hearing summer school: with my wife and two young sons, I was privileged to witness a performance on our main stage given by twenty deaf and twenty hearing kids. They had spent two weeks putting the production together having never met before. They did the staging, lighting, scriptwriting and everything else, and were able to put on a really great performance which kept my lively boys enraptured for nearly an hour; in fact, three weeks later they're still acting out scenes with their friends. That was definitely a bit of theatrical magic for me: to see our young participants working together and communicating with no regard for the differences between them is something that I will never forget and it shows why everyone who works at the Arts is committed to our education and access work. Theatre is a strong and positive force for change and everyone in the community should have a chance to experience and, where possible, participate in the theatrical experience.

Without a doubt, the thing about this job that I find hardest is the reconciliation of artistic possibilities and practical realities. For art and theatre to succeed, there has to be an element of idealism: imagination and an ability to see new ways of doing things are essential parts of the creative process. However, there is only one way to pay the wages of a passionately committed member of staff, and that is to have money in the bank. It is my job to try to present a stimulating, challenging and adventurous programme at the Arts Theatre but, at the same time, to make sure that all involved keep their feet on the ground. I regard it as my responsibility to look after the staff, to make sure that they are rewarded for their efforts and to safeguard the long-term financial health of the Arts for future generations of Cambridge theatre-goers. There is a strong sense of history about the Theatre and I'm very proud to be part of its future.

Maureen Lipman

Peggy for You
by Alan Plater
September, 2000

Who was Peggy Ramsay?

She was a literary agent – and if that sounds a little dry, she was a very juicy literary agent. What is an agent? 'Sordid people,' said Peggy, 'can't stand any of them.' They're enablers, and she enabled British writing – new British drama – to emerge from the miasmic years of the French window. She was fierce and she was feisty, she was funny and she was impossible, she was sexy and she was a great inspiration to people like David Hare, who adored her, and Alan Ayckbourn, who did, too, and Christopher Hampton and Alan Plater, who wrote this play, and Jack Rosenthal, who's seen it a few times. And of course Simon Callow, who had this extraordinary relationship with her which was a love affair without sex between a seventy-year-old woman and a thirty-year-old gay man – but it was nevertheless a sort of courtly love and something they'd both been looking for.

For somebody who claimed as Peggy did that she wanted no publicity, nothing to do with media, she's had three books written about her, she's been played by Vanessa Redgrave in the film *Prick Up Your Ears*, she's been played by me and by Anna Carteret in a play by Peter Nicholls, who was also a client. She left three million pounds for new writers, which was no small biscuit in those days, and she's really in the air, buzzing around, so probably – although she would claim to hate that – I think she's smiling beatifically down. Or up.

You've got first-hand knowledge of her because although you didn't actually meet her, you did have to take some of her famous phone calls as your husband, Jack, was part of her stable.

Yes, and I was very green, I didn't realise this wasn't done. When he sent her a stage play called *Smash*, which in fact we played here at the Cambridge Arts Theatre with Nigel Hawthorne, Stephen Moore and myself, she didn't respond immediately; after eight or nine days she hadn't said anything, so I just phoned her up and said 'he's waiting to hear from you'. Of course, ever after that she called me 'Jack Rosenthal's impossibly ambitious wife' because I was the twin threat – the actress and the wife; she loathed both, apparently. The funny thing about the story is that when we came here to Cambridge with the play, which was very well-received everywhere we went, Peggy was sitting in the stalls telling the producer not to bother bringing it in to London, even though she was Jack's agent – and that's what she was, she had odd loyalties: if she didn't think something that you'd done was right, even though she represented you, she wouldn't push it. So we have things to thank Peggy for and we have things not to thank Peggy for, and I don't suppose for one minute she would have picked me to play this part any more than Joyce Grenfell would have picked me – wrong class, wrong face, wrong looks – but it's to do with the eccentricity of the women: you have to have someone who is prepared to be unattractive as well as attractive, and that requires a certain state of mind; you have to be uncompromising to play Peggy, and not ask for sympathy at all because she wouldn't have wanted it; you have to be as dastardly as she could be, and that's certainly something that I'm prepared to do.

It's a very vocal role but also a very physical one, and one of the finest things about the production is these incredible comic stances; she had a way of moving which was very much her own, didn't she?

When we did the first run-through, the producer, Michael Codron, who of course knew her terribly well – the first thing he said to me was 'you've got the walk, dear', and actually the walk always comes first for me; Beryl Reid said that once you've got the feet right you've got everything, and I think that's true. I saw a snatch of film of Peggy on an *Arena* programme which they did towards the end of her life, and there was film of her walking through those antiquarian arcades in St Martin's Lane which she did at lunchtime – often she'd walk barefoot across London, apparently. She had terrible bunions, although I didn't know this at the time, and this elongated stride which was quite ostrich-like. I also knew from Jack that she constantly flapped and fiddled with her clothes – she wore beautiful clothes which she I'm sure went to Paris for but she told everybody she'd got them from a second-hand shop. She was always fiddling with her bra – although she often didn't wear underwear – and her clothes were never quite in the right place; that's a gift for an actress. She worked in these two tiny constricted offices at the top of a Dickensian flight of stairs and she could hardly swing a kitten round – yet she swung everything round; from the restriction, from the repression came a volcano waiting to erupt, so that when people went in there for the first time some of the stories they came out with were just amazing. I met someone from South Africa who said he spent two hours with her after which he felt he understood exactly what theatre was. He'd gone in because she wouldn't let any plays go to South Africa during the apartheid phase – she was South African and she wouldn't let them have anything. He said he came to London and sat at her feet for two hours, and she was just so fantastic talking about European theatre; at the end, he offered to give all the profits to the ANC if she'd let him do these things in South Africa. She threw him down the stairs.

After watching your performance, Joyce Grenfell's husband said that it was nice to see her again. When you're playing a real person, you obviously pare back all the bits and pieces and rebuild them again to become that person: does Peggy live with you? Do you answer the phone as Peggy Ramsay?

Not really, no, although I drift in and out and, if I'm talking about the play, she comes back in. I think it's a double-edged sword, really, because although I've improved enormously since we opened at Hampstead, quite a lot of the reviews said 'I suppose as an impersonation it's quite good'. In fact, it doesn't matter if it's an impersonation or not because nobody knows her; the point is that I have to get possessed, it's just the way I work, and therefore I think it's quite easy to dismiss the performances that I give as facile because they appear to be impersonations. This tends to happen with people who change enormously; if you go to see some of the great actors and actresses, you see them and that's what they are and that's what you go for; I can't do that – I'd be bored being me even if I knew what me was. I have to get inside and zip up, really; in a sense, it's something the public like more than the critics, but I can't do it any other way.

Alison Steadman, pictured with Bryan Pringle

Entertaining Mr. Sloane
by Joe Orton
September, 2000

What appeals to you most about *Entertaining Mr. Sloane?*

I think this is Joe Orton's best play. It was written in the 1960s, but the audiences find it as fresh today as they did then. We had a chat with the audience after the show last night and it was surprising how many young people there were who'd never heard of Joe Orton and knew nothing about him and were amazed that this play was thirty-something years old. So I don't think it matters whether or not you remember the sixties yourself: if a play's a good play, it's a good play today or thirty years ago and hopefully it'll still be a good play in another thirty years; good plays stand the test of time. It's about human beings and the human condition, and how people find themselves in certain situations and how they cope with them, therefore audiences are fascinated by it: it's a part of life they know nothing about. Also, the writing is very clever because Joe Orton was a poet; this play isn't a naturalistic play, it's heightened realism and it's very black and very funny, and a joy to be in.

As far as TV audiences are concerned, you came to prominence with the wonderful Essex girl, Beverly, in *Abigail's Party*, which was extraordinarily successful.

Yes, and it was strange how we came to do the play for television in the first place. We were at Hampstead Theatre for twelve weeks and the play was a huge success, so they asked us to bring it back after a break of three or four weeks; my husband and I had decided we were going to start a family and it just happened that during that break I found out I was pregnant, and I was delighted. I went back to do the play at Hampstead for twelve weeks, and West End managements were coming and wanting to do it and I had to say I couldn't, so we thought that was that. Then a BBC TV producer came to see the show and loved it, and they had an empty slot because a play had fallen through. It was pure,

pure luck. We went into the studio, and had to cut a bit and change the music, and recorded it. The night it came to be broadcast, there was an ITV strike and all sorts of things were going wrong, and that culminated in an audience of something like nineteen million. It was a huge success and it really took us by surprise, but we were thrilled and amazed. Then I won an *Evening Standard* award for my stage performance, which was another thrill, so there I was sitting at home with my new baby, which was lovely, and an award, and everybody was talking about *Abigail's Party*. In fact, people have never really stopped talking about it.

You also appeared in the ultimate 'bonnet drama' as fussy old Mrs. Bennet; you must have loved that.

I did, but I actually didn't know the book before I was asked to do it. When it came along and I read it, I thought she was such a brilliant character, a woman larger than life, always on the verge of hysteria – and very rightly so when you look at her life with five daughters and the family about to be thrown out on the street without a crust of bread if she doesn't get them married off. You can understand her predicament, but it was great fun to do with lovely locations down in Wiltshire. And it was marvellous to discover Jane Austen: I went to her house and read a lot about her. Recently we toured *Mr Sloane* to Bath which of course is big Jane Austen territory, and I was walking to the Theatre from my digs one day and saw Bennet Street, and I wondered if that's where she'd got the name; it's fascinating to think about, and I wish I could have asked her, but I like to think that she did.

As far as film is concerned, you've recently been in _Topsy Turvey_, which was very different again.

That's just a cameo part but it's quite fun: I play the lady who designed the costumes for _The Mikado_, although when I say 'designed', that's not quite true; she 'assembled' them under Gilbert's instruction. Nobody in Victorian England knew anything about Japan or its customs, and the fashion of the time was to be corseted like mad with an hour-glass figure; that was considered beautiful and the actresses of the day wanted to look as curvaceous as they could. During the research, we found out that when they were asked to wear Japanese costumes that made them appear straight up and down, they went mad; there were terrible rows about it, but Gilbert insisted that they were absolutely authentic and not anglicised in any way. He was quite a taskmaster and oversaw every aspect of the productions, so this poor lady had the unenviable task of being diplomatic and telling the ladies they looked lovely, knowing nothing about Japanese life herself. _The Mikado_ was inspired by a Japanese Fair that was on in London, which told people about the food and so on for the first time; that must have been quite progressive when you think about it, because we haven't had Japanese restaurants in London for that long – perhaps 35 or 40 years. So it was a fascinating job.

Was it a real disappointment to you not to get the part of the mother in _Little Voice_ after you'd done the stage play?

I get asked this a lot, and I've known Brenda [Blethyn] for 25 years and we're friends. When you play a role on stage for the first time and you develop that character with the author, of course you have a sense that it's your part – you can't help it. But once you've finished, the play goes out all around the country and dozens of actresses will play that role to greater or lesser success. It's no longer your part – you have to let it go; I've played Beverly once, but so have thousands of women and when they play it, it belongs to them, that's the nature of the game. I'm sure I've played dozens of parts and maybe not known that some poor actress is sitting at home saying she played it for the first time. That's what happens. I'm not as well known in the film world as Brenda, and these guys that sit making those decisions don't worry about who played it first; they worry about attracting people into the cinema, and it's as plain and simple as that. When I first heard that I didn't get the role, of course I was disappointed, I'd be lying if I said I wasn't, but you have to get over it very quickly and look forward to the future, not dwell on things that you've not done.

Clive Francis

Entertaining Mr. Sloane
by Joe Orton
September, 2000

'On August 9, 1967, 34-year-old Joe Orton was battered to death with a hammer. His head had been so severely beaten that it was concave, like a punctured grapefruit. The murderer, his 41-year-old lover, Kenneth Halliwell, lay sprawled on the floor next to him having committed suicide by swallowing a bottle of Nembutal. For Orton it was the end of a short but brilliant career.

'Four days after this horrific event, I sat alongside Sheila Hancock and Edward Woodward in a rehearsal room in north London. We were beginning work on a television version of *Entertaining Mr Sloane,* the Orton play that I re-launched at [London's] Arts Theatre, where it first appeared. The writer's chair sat empty next to us. The mood was sombre, the occasion feeling like a macabre epitaph to his edgy, uncomfortable gifts.

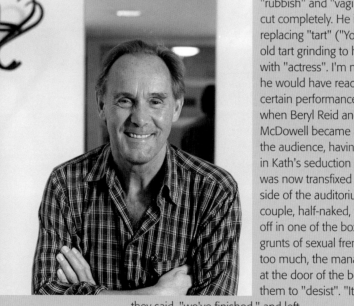

'The script was the last thing Orton worked on. He had trimmed the play neatly down to ninety minutes, a precise and clever piece of adaptation. Various sections were rewritten and a number of very funny lines inserted.

'This powerful play exploded on the West End stage at a time when the Lord Chamberlain was still wielding a blue pencil against anything that might upset the morals of his sensitive flock. My first West End appearance, in *There's a Girl in My Soup* (1966), had come under attack. As I staggered on stage with an appalling hangover, I had to say, "my eyes feel like two piss-holes in the snow." This was changed, at the Chamberlain's insistence, to "rissoles". So it's hard to imagine how, two years earlier, *Mr Sloane,* the most shocking play of its day, ever made it to the West End.'

Nonetheless, his Lordship looked down his nose at certain references. For "arse", "harris" had to be substituted; "shit" had to be changed to "rubbish" and "vaginalatrous" cut completely. He insisted on replacing "tart" ("You're like an old tart grinding to her climax") with "actress". I'm not sure how he would have reacted to a certain performance in 1975, when Beryl Reid and Malcolm McDowell became aware that the audience, having lost interest in Kath's seduction of Sloane, was now transfixed by the other side of the auditorium, where a couple, half-naked, were having it off in one of the boxes. When the grunts of sexual frenzy became too much, the manager tapped at the door of the box and asked them to "desist". "It's all right," they said, "we've finished," and left.

'Orton was bemused by the Lord Chamberlain's attitude to his play. "The funny thing about the Lord Chamberlain," he said, "was that he cut all the hetero-sexual bits and kept all the homosexual ones." (Although homosexuality was rife during the Sixties, it was still a criminal offence at the time.) For instance, Ed, when talking about the crudeness of women, assures Sloane that, "It's a thing you grow out of. With me behind you, boy, you'll grow out of it." But then Orton was the master of the innuendo, writing about sex obliquely rather than aiming it directly at you.

'According to *Prick Up Your Ears*, John Lahr's brilliant study of Orton, *Entertaining Mr Sloane* is the most autobiographical of his plays, the story of a young lad's dream of the ideal family, "in which he is never excluded and always needed." The story is based on fact. Orton's mother Elsie became obsessed by the arrival of a young lodger, a lorry driver, so much so that she was forever spring-cleaning the house and pandering to him. Eventually the family persuaded him to go, leaving behind the germ of a plot, which the young Orton seized upon.

'Mr Sloane, the role I played on television, "has to be lethal and charming," Orton said, "a combination of magical black-leather meanness and boyish innocence. What many people have found difficult to understand about him is the combination of innocence and amorality. The English always tend to equate innocence with ignorance, which is nonsense." He summed the play up by saying, "*Entertaining Mr Sloane* is a comedy in so far as the whole human situation is comic and farcical."

'The play opened at the New Arts Theatre on May 6, 1964, to mixed notices. "Not for a long time have I disliked a play so much," wrote *The Daily Telegraph's* critic, WA Darlington. "I feel as if snakes had been writhing around my feet." Not one to miss an opportunity, Orton began writing letters to the *Telegraph* under an assortment of pseudonyms, some expressing disgust (most famously Mrs Edna Welthorpe), others supporting the maligned playwright.

'Playwright Sean O'Casey saw *Entertaining Mr Sloane* as a play "to make a man pull his trousers up", and *Sunday Times* critic Harold Hobson as "a vision of total evil". He went on to say that Orton reminded him a lot of Jane Austen! Terence Rattigan, then regarded as a rather dated figure, considered it to be the most exciting first play he had seen in thirty years. "I saw Wilde [in your play]," he wrote, ". . . in some ways better, because it had more bite. *Sloane* mustn't die at the Arts."

'And thanks to Rattigan's campaigning, it didn't. *Entertaining Mr Sloane* transferred to Wyndham's Theatre on June 29, 1964, and Joe Orton's short reign as a West End playwright began. Towards the end of 1997 I managed to get hold of a copy of the television version which I had done 30 years earlier. Watching it again, I realised what an extraordinary piece it was. In many ways before its time, and not in the least dated, it seems as relevant now as it was when it first appeared.

'*Entertaining Mr Sloane* is still a disturbing and funny play, one that I'm proud to be part of.'

This article first appeared in the *Daily Telegraph* on 22nd January 2001.

Susan Hampshire

Relatively Speaking
by Alan Ayckbourn
November, 2000

Not even public transport can ruffle Susan Hampshire. 'I love it when a train is late because you suddenly have half an hour you didn't expect,' admits the actress who put costume drama on the map in the sixties and seventies, gave up acting to marry and write in the eighties, and gained a legion of new fans in the nineties with the television hits *The Grand* and *Monarch of the Glen*. 'After you've cleaned out your handbag, sorted your diary, written the odd letter and paid a few cheques, you've finally got twenty minutes to yourself.'

It's not surprising that Hampshire empties her handbag on the move: she's not just a prolific and hard-working actress, but a champion for dyslexia and an executive committee member of the charity Population Concern as well. It wasn't the career she had in mind; from the age of three, she trained to be a classical ballet dancer at her mother's Knightsbridge dance school but, by fifteen, was too tall. 'I didn't have the perfect instep, I didn't have the perfect turn-out – in fact, I didn't have anything you need to be a ballet dancer! Seeing what dancers go through now, I was lucky. We think there's not enough work for actors, but for dancers it's far worse.'

The switch to theatre came about by accident, after she was approached on the underground and asked to do a screen test to play a young Jean Simmons. 'I had to learn some lines, and my mother sewed a nightie for the test. I got the part, and being a child of seven in a film where people treat you as if you're something special was like tasting blood: I never forgot it. Although I put it from my mind and carried on wanting to be a dancer or a nurse, somewhere lurked

that wonderful feeling I had when I was being spoiled as an actress. Then I had funny parts in school plays and people laughed, and I remember it being a real buzz because I wasn't very good at history or algebra, but that went rather well.' When nursing was also ruled out because she couldn't do the equivalent of a Latin O-level, Hampshire sat down with her brother-in-law and wrote to a hundred repertory companies, eventually landing a job on the pier at Bognor Regis as an assistant stage manager.

On a salary of just £5.50 a week, which meant a diet of carrots, scraps of liver and invitations to Sunday lunch, Hampshire had the time of her life. 'Because I hadn't been to drama school, I had a lot of rough edges to be knocked off, but there were no responsibilities other than to be a good ASM and do the small parts I got as well as I could. I felt so carefree: I had a bicycle to collect props and I was dreadfully bad in every play without exception – you could hear people in the front row saying "oh, she's no better this week". But it didn't matter because it was such a wonderful feeling to work in the theatre.'

Despite the string of stage and screen hits that she now has to her name, Hampshire has had to work hard to overcome difficulties which would have put an end to the career of a less determined lady. Her dyslexia, which makes learning lines a constant uphill battle, went undiagnosed until she was thirty. 'I always knew that I was a poor reader, and when I was very young, they thought I was mentally retarded,' she recalls. 'I had an extremely supportive mother, a very kind brother and two sisters, all of whom helped me, and I made very good friends at school; I'd do things like clean out their satchel' – it's that handbag thing again – 'and they'd help

me with prep.' Although Hampshire found ways around the panic and fear involved in not being able to identify letters or numbers, the process of learning a significant role was something else altogether. 'Early on, even though I knew acting didn't quite mean standing up and saying whatever you wanted, I had no idea that I'd be expected to wade through twelve scripts at a time. Over the years, I've devised my own way of doing it, which is to allow masses of time: what takes you fifteen minutes to learn will take me two hours. Nowadays, I always learn my lines pretty well before I start rehearsals, otherwise I make such a fool of myself at the first reading. I pretend to read, but in fact it's already there.'

Hampshire has starred in some of the most popular British television series ever made, winning Emmy awards for her roles as Fleur in *The Forsyte Saga*, Becky Sharp in *Vanity Fair*, and Sarah in *The First Churchills*. 'It was almost like doing live television. We only had an evening in which to record the whole hour-long episode, so I'd finish a scene, get changed with the tape still running, rush back on slightly flushed and out of breath, and continue as if it were three days later. The filming was done out of sequence, so in the morning you'd be a seventeen-year-old and by the afternoon you were forty-five. In *Vanity Fair*, which was the first colour series, they had to paint us slightly green because the cameras were picking up too much red! Television is slightly easier now, but it isn't quite as magical: you have ten big hit series and the same actors get employed year after year, and young people are coming up and not getting the opportunities they should be. It's a much tougher world for young actors these days.'

In the early 1980s, Hampshire disappeared from the screen – 'I was in my forties and that's not an easy time for female actresses' – to marry and write books on gardening and dyslexia. She returned with a vengeance in more period dramas: *Coming Home* and its sequel, *Nancherrow*, in which she appeared alongside Joanna Lumley and Donald Sinden; and *The Grand*, where she stole the show as a retired Madame. 'Esme was just an old tart but great to play,' she says. 'I used to wait as if it were Christmas to open the scripts each week. Some people were shocked that I played such a part and said it must have been awful to look so old, but the more parts I play looking older, the easier it is to work. I can't pretend I'm young again.'

Most recently, she has introduced herself to a whole new generation as Molly in *Monarch of the Glen*, set in the heart of the Highlands; the filming, which means spending five months in extreme isolation, is a labour of love. 'It's a twelve hour journey door-to-door, and we all live together in a lodge – it's back to bed-sit time. There are no cinemas, it's over an hour to the nearest restaurant, and you don't see a house – in fact, you don't see anything except the odd sheep. But the air and countryside are breathtakingly beautiful and we're surrounded by calm, albeit with a slightly melancholy feel from the battles and bloodshed that have taken place nearby. It's a long time to be away from home, but I like Molly enormously, particularly the fact that she gambles – she's got this wild streak…a little flirtatious and slightly barmy.'

Susan Hampshire may share some of Molly's wilder eccentricities – her idea of the perfect day off is to jump on Eurostar and lunch in Paris – but she has a tough, uncompromisingly caring side that could not be further from her more glamorous screen roles. Through her involvement with Population Concern, she has visited Vietnamese refugee camps in Hong Kong and slums in Bangladesh, where she has helped to empower women in some of the poorest areas of the world. 'India's a seductive country. When you're there, you see enormous poverty which is endured with such a good nature that you wonder if they know something that we in the west don't; there's so much suffering, but they don't cry and they don't complain, and you come back not knowing quite how to cope with your life. The plight of the woman is a tough one: they have no rights and they're not educated, so Population Concern offers them skills, helps their children and gives them good health care. In Britain, we have the highest rate of unwanted pregnancies in Europe, so we're not in a position to dictate, but we can say here's some help if you want to take it.'

Sir Derek Jacobi

God Only Knows
by Hugh Whitemore
October, 2000

Many people's earliest memories of you go back to the wonderful *I Claudius* – was that fun to make?

Yes it was, and it was very special to me, not only because it was a wonderful part with a wonderful company and director, but because it opened so many doors for me. I'd been an actor for sixteen years by the time I played Claudius, ten of them with the National Theatre, but I could have been with the National Coal Board for all that people knew of me. Suddenly, there I was on TV being fed into people's homes every week for six months; what was particularly wonderful was that I became known in America, so I could work there as well, and it had long been an ambition for me to perform on stage in the States. It was enormously valuable – and it's very much part of me.

We've seen you in a toga again recently, but this time on the big screen: did you get a sense of the epic nature of *Gladiator* while you were making it?

Very much so. We filmed it all on the island of Malta and the sets were simply astonishing: they created half the Coliseum to scale, and to stand in that arena was extraordinary because it was like the real thing, and all the sets outside the Coliseum were true to scale so you felt like a little ant and you just knew it was going to look amazing. The other half was added on by computer later, and with digital techniques they could add thousands to the crowd very easily, although there were 2,500 real Maltese people out there boiling in the sun each day. It was very exciting, although I didn't realise at the time that it would be quite the hit it has been. Because it's an action movie, a lot was cut, including three of my scenes – but there was enough left!

So are you enjoying being back in the theatre?

They can't cut me out there! Absolutely. I've recently done a production of *Uncle Vanya* on Broadway, and that was the first play I'd done in four years. I deliberately did that to get my feet back in the water before *God Only Knows*, because four years is a long time to be away and theatre is a very special technique, quite unlike anything to do with the camera and much more frightening, much more difficult. I think I'm back in the harness now, but this is a testing role: it's an enormous part and has been a real pig to learn – lots of blood, sweat and tears – but it's fascinating.

You've had some fantastic roles – which stand out in particular for you?

Several really. I suppose Hamlet, which I've played many, many times on stage and screen. Certainly Cyrano de Bergerac, Alan Turing in Hugh Whitemore's play *Breaking the Code*. But I've been very blessed in my career, I've had some lovely parts and they've nearly all stayed with me.

And you're no stranger to Cambridge or to the Arts Theatre.

No, I was at St John's from 1957 to 1960 and I've been wandering round in a haze of nostalgia all week because I've only been back about twice in the forty years since I left. Lots of things aren't here any more – the Whim Coffee shop and the Kohinoor just opposite St John's, where I spent many an evening. I'm talking in terms of restaurants and cafés, but shops, too, like Joshua Taylor. Oh, and the Dorothy Ballroom! But basically it's all there, which is lovely. I wandered around John's today, actually – a bit weepy, feeling a bit old.

But fond memories?

Oh very fond, particularly of the Arts Theatre because a great chum of mine, Judy Birdwood, was the wardrobe mistress and she lived in a house next to the stage door – I think it's now a bookshop; I spent nearly all my three years as an undergraduate in that house until she moved from there to a house in Portugal Place. But I have great memories of Cambridge – it was a magic, magic time.

Jean Boht

Jack and the Beanstalk
December, 2000 –
January 2001

I was brought up in the Wirral near Liverpool, but Liverpool was bombed very heavily in 1941 and we had very little in those years: we didn't think about getting much for Christmas – an orange, an apple and a bag of chocolate coins if you were lucky – because there was sweet rationing. But we had a lot of fun, and we made decorations out of paper and newspaper and decorated the house; there was a tree and I remember that my grandmother's decorations were so beautiful; she had very treasured things made of coloured glass that she'd saved over many, many years.

We spent a lot of Christmases with her, away from the bombing, and I remember one very funny year when we'd gone down on the train to Nottingham in the middle of the night and were bundled off to bed as soon as we got there. When I opened my stocking in the morning – I must have been all of five years old at the time – there was a watch, and I couldn't believe how lucky I was because I hadn't asked Father Christmas for anything like that. So I bandied this watch around all day, and then I suddenly noticed that my cousin Pat seemed a bit depressed; she, of course, had indeed asked Father Christmas for a watch but didn't get it; instead, she'd got whatever I was supposed to have. Gradually, the family started to ask if they could have a look at it, but I wasn't going to part with it; eventually, they had to say that Father Christmas had made a terrible mistake and had put Pat's watch in the wrong stocking, and that I could have one later. They must have wrestled it off me, because it was given to Pat, who cheered up no end!

So there we were in this wonderful Victorian house in Nottingham, with an enormous table which would seat about 24 people and which had a middle section that was only ever pulled out for Christmas day. It had a big handle and, as children, we'd sit on the table while our fathers or brothers – although a lot of them were away at sea during the war – would unwind the handle and put the middle section in. All the wives used to get really cheesed off because my grandmother was a great martinet and they were all expected to cook on a really old-fashioned range and work very hard to get Christmas lunch on; they were always exhausted by the time it was ready, but we thought it was all wonderful.

Then we'd all sit in the front parlour – and there was a proper Victorian parlour in those days which was only used on Sundays – and sing songs and play games. We didn't seem to have very much, but I had wonderful fun with my cousins. Nottingham seemed to have escaped the bombing, so we were sent down there for some sort of safety: it was always magic, because I really believed in Father Christmas and I can't remember a time when I didn't – I think I still do!

Isla Blair and Julian Glover

In Praise of Love
by Terence Rattigan
January – February, 2001

Max Stafford-Clark and Out of Joint

Rita, Sue and Bob Too
by Andrea Dunbar, Bradford 1982
A State Affair
by Robin Soans, Bradford 2000
February, 2001

'**M**y first term as the Royal Court's Artistic Director began in January 1980 and one way of becoming immediately involved in the grass-roots was through the annual Young Writers' Festival. This was a national competition open to any aspiring writer up to the age of eighteen. Plays by younger writers made particularly strenuous demands on the actors' versatility. Talking cabbages featured in one play and neurotic guinea pigs in another, while adolescence provoked a flood of gloomy dramas that invariably ended in suicide or unwanted pregnancies.

'But in early 1980 there was one outstanding play. Written boldly in green biro on pages ripped from a school exercise book, it told the story of a Bradford schoolgirl who became pregnant on the night she lost her virginity. A family argument was depicted with brutal authenticity, and the final scene was heartbreakingly affecting and bleak. The principal character, just called "Girl", had lost her baby and by accident met the boy who had made her pregnant. The innocence of the mutual recriminations revealed how young the protagonists really were. I tried to get in touch with the writer, whose name was Andrea Dunbar, but she was in a battered wives' home in Keighley and communication was difficult.

'A pack of abandoned and feral dogs roamed the centre of Brafferton Arbor, the crescent on which Andrea lived. The pastoral name was misleading: it was bleak. Some houses were boarded up, and some gardens were a tangled mess of grass and weeds often featuring bits of car engine mounted on breeze blocks. Like the occasional battered caravan that also blossomed in some gardens, they were

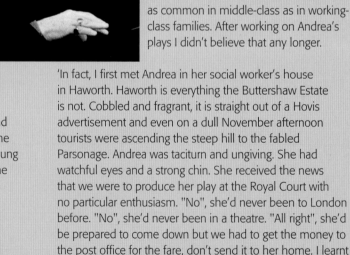

dreams of escape – hopeless male fantasies doomed to remain for ever in a state of incompletion. Andrea's own father had stayed with his family and his violence and feckless drinking had been the dramatic centre of Andrea's childhood. Even in 1980 this was unusual: in most families the father had fucked off. With no work and no possibility of being a provider, men had become redundant in every sense of the word. Families scratched by on benefits, on the occasional odd job, on petty crime and on dole fraud. The poverty was shocking. So were other things. A friend of Andrea's on the Arbor had had a baby by her uncle and it had been born with a skin disease. Andrea related the details with an amused horror. Correct political thinking would have it that male violence and abusive uncles are as common in middle-class as in working-class families. After working on Andrea's plays I didn't believe that any longer.

'In fact, I first met Andrea in her social worker's house in Haworth. Haworth is everything the Buttershaw Estate is not. Cobbled and fragrant, it is straight out of a Hovis advertisement and even on a dull November afternoon tourists were ascending the steep hill to the fabled Parsonage. Andrea was taciturn and ungiving. She had watchful eyes and a strong chin. She received the news that we were to produce her play at the Royal Court with no particular enthusiasm. "No", she'd never been to London before. "No", she'd never been in a theatre. "All right", she'd be prepared to come down but we had to get the money to the post office for the fare, don't send it to her home. I learnt that it was a culture where you didn't give yourself away. Admitting to pain or showing enthusiasm were equally undesirable. You had to be hard. And Andrea had developed a stoicism and a stubbornness that were impermeable and particular.

'But she enjoyed rehearsal and was amazed to find how much she laughed at the scenes she had written. "It weren't so funny when it were happening," she commented wryly about a neighbourhood row that escalated into a riot. Somehow the alchemy of theatre often turned her scenes into something that was hilarious as well as brutal. Humour co-existed with anger and desperation. Andrea and a friend came to stay while the play was being rehearsed. It was a long way from Brafferton Arbor to Gloucester Crescent and both of us had to adapt. She didn't like food much and found mange tout particularly disgusting. And I found it strange to cope with a writer who was more enthusiastic about going to Buckingham Palace or Madame Tussaud's than about coming to rehearsal. But her comments were apt and incisive: "He weren't sitting down, he were standing up when he said that," she would say. Or, "She didn't laugh then but she did laugh when she said that." The auto-biographical nature of the play and Andrea's gift of total recall meant she could add lines or develop an argument as we were rehearsing. I badgered her for more detail and invariably she provided it.

'The play did well…After *The Arbor* Andrea went back to Bradford and began to write a second play. She had no desire to move away from Buttershaw and had little curiosity about life elsewhere. She started writing again and phoned a couple of times to ask "What can you do on stage?" She wasn't seeking advice about Brecht, but was asking how sexually candid it was possible to be in the theatre.

'*Rita, Sue and Bob Too* was Andrea's second play and it became notorious for the hilarious first scene in which two schoolgirl babysitters take it in turns to have sex with their employer in the back of his car. There's an increase in confidence, and although there's never much political analysis in Andrea's work, there's an awareness of life getting grimmer…But the hardness of the life is mitigated by the sheer priapic vigour of the two girls who certainly don't see themselves as victims. "I hope he brings us here again," says Rita anxiously at the end of their first sex session. "Oh he will. Make no mistake about it," says Sue with confidence. It's the one certainty in a fickle world.

'Andrea died of a brain haemorrhage at the age of twenty-nine. She had written three plays and she had had three children. All her plays are written from a young woman's perspective, but as her technique sharpened she began to move away from the simple autobiographical stance of *The Arbor*, and in *Shirley*, her final play, there are several scenes written from the point of view of the older woman character, who in previous plays was just called "Mother". Her plays as a girl showed an extraordinary talent, the tragedy is that she never lived to write the plays of her maturity. Script meetings at the Royal Court throw up lots of ideas which aren't always followed up. One was a season of work entitled "Dead Young". It was to have been devoted to the work of playwrights who had died under the age of thirty. Andrea would have taken a place alongside Büchner (twenty-four), Farquhar (twenty-nine) and Marlowe (twenty-nine).'

Max Stafford-Clark, August 2000.
Taken from the introduction to the play-text of *Rita, Sue and Bob Too* and *A State Affair,* published by Methuen.

George Rylands

Chairman of the Arts Theatre Trust,
1946–1982

The name of George Humphrey Wolferstan Rylands, CBE – or Dadie, as he was more affectionately known – is as inextricably linked with the history and character of Cambridge Arts Theatre as that of Keynes. Imaginative and dedicated, Dadie's contribution to the longevity of the Arts was twofold: as an actor and director with the Marlowe Society, he brought to its stage a series of remarkable classical productions, nurturing the talent and driving forward the ambitions of many of the country's most celebrated actors, directors and broadcasters; as Chairman of the Arts Theatre Trust for nearly forty years, he proved to be an inspirational leader in years of financial uncertainty, spearheading – and personally contributing to – a number of fundraising campaigns and doggedly garnering the support of an often contrary audience.

Dadie was born in 1902, and went up to King's College, Cambridge from Eton in January 1921, where he studied first Classics and then English, taking a starred First. During his undergraduate days, he was President of the Amateur Dramatic Club and acted in a number of the Marlowe Dramatic Society's productions. On going down from University, he lived for a time near the Keynes' London home and made many friends in Bloomsbury, including the Strachey family, Duncan Grant and Vanessa Bell; he joined Leonard and Virginia Woolf at the Hogarth Press while writing his Fellowship dissertation and, in 1927, was elected to King's College as a Fellow, becoming involved with Keynes in a number of innovative programmes.

From the early 1930s, the Arts Theatre project became his main concern outside College matters, but he also continued to play a leading role in guiding the ADC and The Marlowe Dramatic Society, to which he devoted more than forty years' service. His many notable Marlowe productions became famous for their musical clarity and attention to the rhythms of language, and he received significant critical acclaim: writing in *The New Statesman and Nation*, the novelist Elizabeth Bowen said of his 1938 production of *King Lear,* 'The tragedy could not have been more fully realised, or played with greater lucidity…these performances did *King Lear* a great service: they offered an unobstructed channel for the rush of the play.'; the following year, the *New Statesman* summed up Dadie's singular talent for reaching an audience in its praise of his Jacobite setting of *Macbeth:* 'one cannot be too grateful to the anonymous producer and actors, who, instead of massacring the play to make a holiday for themselves, attempted so successfully to place us directly in contact with the meaning and beauty of Shakespeare's text.'

Unquestionably, the Arts Theatre benefited considerably from Dadie's many professional engagements outside Cambridge, engagements which brought some fine productions to the city's stage: the first of these was a 1944 *Hamlet* for Tennent in which a cast of John Gielgud, Leslie Banks, Francis Lister and Peggy Ashcroft gave a week of performances at the Arts prior to a long run in the glamorous Haymarket Theatre season; the head of

This page and previous: George 'Dadie' Rylands photographed on his 80th birthday in 1982

the Tennent Organisation, Hugh Beaumont, provides a telling insight into early rehearsals: 'When Rylands first met the cast it was reminiscent of a new boy arriving at his first prep school, but within forty eight hours the cast were skipping around like a squad of recruits under a strict sergeant-major'. Based on fifteen years' experience in the role, some thought of this as Gielgud's most accomplished Hamlet and, in the 1950s, Dadie was instrumental in another of his friend's great hits when he helped Gielgud to adapt some lectures into *The Ages of Man*, a recital which became the most successful of all Shakespearean solo shows.

Dadie never let the considerable demands of his role as University Lecturer in English, nor his many other college offices, get in the way of his devotion to theatre, particularly to the Arts. He chaired the Apollo Society, oversaw the recording of the complete works of Shakespeare for the British Council and was a Director of the Old Vic; more recently, his influence on British theatre has continued to spread through the work of three undergraduate protégés, Peter Hall, Trevor Nunn and John Barton. Moreover, he was Chairman of the Arts Theatre Trust right up until his eightieth birthday in 1982 and remained active in the Theatre's fortunes even beyond that: the last show he ever directed – at the age of 83 – was a fund-raising gala to mark the fiftieth anniversary of the Arts Theatre in 1986; compered by Richard Baker, the evening starred Peggy Ashcroft, Judi Dench, Michael Williams, Ian McKellen, Eleanor Bron, Derek Jacobi, Peter Hall, Daniel Massey, Prunella Scales, Timothy West, Arthur Marshall, Clive Swift, Richard Pasco, Michael Pennington, Irene Worth, Tony Church, Barbara Leigh-Hunt, Peter Woodthorpe and Trevor Nunn – just some of the figures to whom he had been an inspiration, taking to the very stage which he had done so much to support.

When was the first time you saw something here at the Festival Theatre?

What I remember most is the great season when Flora Robson and Robert Donat acted the leading parts. Tony Guthrie – before he'd made his name – directed a production of *Measure for Measure* here in which Flora played Isabella; I knew Tony, of course, and he was a very brilliant director. Flora's great performance, though, was in

a Victorian melodrama called *Lady Audley's Secret*, a best-seller by Mary Braddon which had caused a sensation in its day and which was then turned into a play. Flora starred in it and they put in a few comic songs; there was a scene where she had to push Lord Audley down a well, and it was very delightful because it showed that Flora wasn't only what she would become – a great tragic actress – but that she could also be a tremendous comedian.

You were here last as a director with the Marlowe Society in 1934.

Yes, that's right, with *Antony and Cleopatra* after the ADC had burnt down. My pupil, Dick David, who sadly died recently, was Antony, and Frances Rowe, who was very remarkable as an undergraduate actress, was Cleopatra; it was the first time that the girls had been allowed by Newnham and Girton to take part, and therefore I was able to do the play I'd most wanted to do – *Antony and Cleopatra*. Up until then, all the women's parts had been taken by the men; I'd had a series of female roles as an undergraduate and when I came back as a Fellow – Regan, the Duchess of Malfi, Volumnia in *Coriolanus* – but I was not prepared to do Cleopatra with a boy, that would have been a bit much; you could do it quite well actually with a younger boy, but not with an undergraduate. So I'd waited and waited and waited and then, owing to the Mummers being started, we were finally allowed to have the girls. Frances went on to take part in *The Winter's Tale* and, after that, the girls had it all their own way – quite rightly!

It must be very special for you to be here today and know that the next production here at the Festival Theatre is going to be a Marlowe student production.

Yes, it's very thrilling. The first production of the Marlowe Society in which I took part was an Elizabethan thriller full of murder and adultery called *The Tragedy of Mr Arden of Feversham*, by an unknown author; I acted in that during my first summer here, the summer of 1921, and that was a great excitement. The next one was the very famous Marlowe production of *Troilus and Cressida*. From that point on, I was in most of them until I gave up acting in them to direct them. I hope this *Lady of Pleasure* is going to be a triumphant production – it'll be an education, anyway!

Simon Godwin and The Marlowe Society

Romeo and Juliet
by William Shakespeare
March, 2001

The Marlowe Society was founded by undergraduates in 1907, according to principles espoused by the actor, director and polemicist William Poel, whose productions for the Elizabethan Stage Society had been lauded by Bernard Shaw and would later inspire Nugent Monk's Maddermarket Theatre, as well as the Shakespeare *Prefaces* of Harley Granville Barker. The Society's first production was Marlowe's *Dr Faustus,* a play which it revived in 1951 as part of the Festival of Britain celebrations, prompting this letter to *The Cambridge Review:*

'It is strange how it always seems to be believed that Rupert Brooke was the founder of the Marlowe Society,' Frances Cornford wrote. 'Actually it was founded by Justin Brooke, of Emmanuel, who was a close friend of Rupert Brooke's, though no relation. Justin Brooke came up fresh from Bedales with an enthusiastic understanding of Elizabethan drama, unique for a school-boy, above all in those days. He and some intimate friends thrashed out the conception of The Marlowe Society, which was then revolutionary...

'*Faustus* was the Marlowe's first venture, produced by Justin Brooke in November 1907. He himself took the part of Faustus. By this time Rupert Brooke was a member of the Society, and he played Mephistopheles. Justin Brooke insisted that Rupert Brooke should be the first president, as he himself was going down in 1908, and he was convinced that continuity was important.

'It surely ought to be recognised that all the dramatic experience, enthusiasm and business enterprise which created the Marlowe Society came from Justin Brooke. Because he did not pursue the drama but is now a well-known and enthusiastic Suffolk fruit-farmer, the Marlowe Society should not forget that it owes its existence to him.'

Whatever the disputes surrounding its origins, few would contest the fact that, as it approaches its centenary year, The Marlowe Society has been responsible for some of the most pioneering productions to have graced the Arts Theatre's programme, thanks in no small part to the influence of George Rylands; its contribution to the history of the stage cannot be over-estimated. As Rylands noted, the Marlowe's annual productions of Elizabethan-Jacobean revivals were responsible for putting many a neglected masterpiece back on the map: Shakespeare's *Troilus and Cressida* was unperformed and misunderstood until the Marlowe's legendary 1922 production, and Webster and Jonson have also been restored to the professional canon as a result of the Society's interest in their work.

The Arts Theatre has been home to the Marlowe's annual production since 1936, and the winning combination of professional guidance and student experimentation has been instrumental in starting the careers of a string of fine actors and directors. There have been many memorable productions during that time: a *Duchess of Malfi* in 1942 induced Peggy Ashcroft to take the part in the West End, directed each time by George Rylands; *The White Devil* and *Measure for Measure* went to Berlin in 1948 in the Foreign Office's cultural

'air-lift'; John Barton's 1952 *Julius Caesar* was given in Elizabethan conditions and pronunciation; a *Romeo and Juliet* with Barton as Mercutio and Peter Hall as Tybalt transferred to the Scala, where it was seen by Winston Churchill; Barton's two parts of *Henry IV* starred Ian McKellen, Derek Jacobi and Clive Swift; the 1958 *Edward II* with Jacobi was broadcast by the BBC; Trevor Nunn's 1962 *Macbeth* transferred to a giant theatre in Newcastle; and Griff Rhys Jones' 1977 *Bartholomew Fair* and Sam Mendes' *Cyrano* of 1988 were hugely energetic shows which played to enthusiastic audiences every night.

To this day, the Marlowe Society celebrates clarity in its verse-speaking, intelligence in its acting and direction, and the values of ensemble playing: the result is an annual event which remains challenging, imaginative and new.

'I started off as an actor, only I found I was only ever cast as the posh twit, which was really rather limiting. In the end, Cambridge made me a director. I think if I hadn't been to Cambridge, I would still be pursuing an acting career. Coming back here as a director is strange – the drama scene hasn't changed at all – but the best thing about it is the chance to work with student actors who are still fearless.

One of the most fascinating things you can do as a director is to take a classic play and produce it in a style which is still applicable to audiences today. *Romeo and Juliet* has the status of a fable. It is deeply entrenched in our collective unconsciousness. Yet Shakespeare always has something extra up his sleeve. When we think we know him best, he turns round and draws yet another rabbit out of his seemingly bottomless hat.

So every production seeks to find something new. It's very easy to perform Shakespeare without thinking about the meaning of everything you are saying, but our aim with a young cast has been to uncover the play's lightness of tone; its quicksilver, mercurial quality. Our setting is one of transition. Our period is the 1950s, a time when Italy was in the throes of change, at once struggling to confront the legacy of the Second World War, whilst seeking to redefine itself as a modern state. Against this backdrop, the love affair of Romeo and Juliet is played out, offering the chance of redemption and reintegration.

Influenced by the distant echoes of the films of Fellini, and all the rough magic of his early work, our intention has been to create a fairytale with a political edge; a story embedded in a real world, that reaches out to touch us all today.'

Simon Godwin
Director of the Marlowe's 2001 production of
Romeo and Juliet

Graham Seed

Confusions
by Alan Ayckbourn
April, 2001

You're master of Lower Loxley in Britain's best-loved radio programme; *The Archers* is an institution – does it feel like that to you?

Oh, yes it does – half of me is Nigel Pargeter, I'm afraid. He's part of my life but he's not my complete life, and as an actor I work very hard to make sure I do other things. You have to care about a character, and I think the secret of any soap is to make your character interesting – you can only do that if you defend his corner. So I'm very fond of Nigel and Nigel is nice, but there's a little bit in me that likes to play nasty, unpleasant people and *Confusions* gives me a great chance to show off and be an actor again.

How did you get the part of Nigel?

There's always luck in every job, and I was at the Birmingham Rep many years ago doing a Bernard Shaw play called *Major Barbara*; Vanessa Whitburn, who was then a director, saw me. I was playing an upper class twit – I've played a lot of those – a sort of silly ass, and she told me they were holding auditions that week for *The Archers*. I'd never listened to the programme, but I had a free day so I went along. I was told the part would only be for two weeks, but I got the job and I'm still in the programme.

Is it difficult to work on *The Archers* and do other things at the same time?

You have to have a loyalty to the programme, but there is no contract. As long as you're fair with them and tell them when you've been offered a tour or something, they fit your recordings in around it.

How far in advance is the recording done?

About five weeks. You never really know with *The Archers* how the storylines are going to go, because it's a big cast and sometimes you can have a lean three or four months. Fingers crossed, Nigel isn't forgotten for long.

Do you ever worry that you'll go the way of poor old Walter Gabriel and find a fallen tree in the script?

Is that what happened to Walter Gabriel?! Yes, you always live in fear that something ghastly will happen because it's kept a secret until the very last moment.

Most actors who appear in soaps find them difficult to shake off when they leave; you've played some leading characters, in *Crossroads* and *Brookside* as well as in *The Archers* – how have you escaped the soap trap?

I don't know. Now I'm older, I'm playing more interesting roles in the theatre, and the joy of *The Archers* is that it's only the voice. I don't like being seen as Nigel; I don't know what he looks like, but I always imagine him to be younger, blonde and rather chinless! I really try to play theatre roles that aren't like him in the slightest.

You've appeared in *I Claudius, Gandhi* and *Brideshead Revisited* – wonderful credits on the big and small screens.

I cherished *Brideshead*. I had a wonderful part with John Gielgud – just a cameo, but very funny. I'm a character actor – I wish I were a handsome leading man but I'm not – and I have a distinctive voice, which I can't help.

Gandhi **must have been magnificent and hugely memorable – what's it like to work on something of that scale?**

Terribly exciting. I only had three lines, one of which was 'India's full of grief, old man', which was a nice line to say. I remember being very nervous, arriving on this set just outside New Delhi, and Sir Richard Attenborough said 'thank you for coming all this way'! He had this knack of making all the actors feel at home and wanted, because when you play small parts in huge epics you're just a small cog.

Period pieces – *Brideshead, Jeeves and Wooster* **– feature heavily in your work; do you think those inter-war dramas suit you?**

Yes, it's the voice: I can turn on the 1930s bit! Some actors are very contemporary, and I'm not except for Ayckbourn, which I have a lot of experience of. Certainly the majority of my film and TV work – except for togas in *I Claudius* – has been stiff collars and putting on the studs. I think I became an actor to dress up!

What would you like to do if you had an open contract?

A good sitcom, because I love comedy, and a bit more film and TV. That sounds terribly greedy because – touch wood – I've been very lucky as an actor in having regular work, and that's the important thing, isn't it?

Sir Antony Sher

In conversation with Mandy Morton on the launch of
his autobiography, *Beside Myself.*
May, 2001

Right from the start of this amazing book, it's clear that you weren't exactly born and blessed with the most perfect attributes for an easy life as an actor – South African, gay and Jewish, and all of this in the 1960s.

That's right. My grandparents all came from Eastern Europe at the turn of the century, fleeing the pogroms of that time, and ended up in South Africa where fate played a curious game with them: having been the underdogs in Lithuania, suddenly they were able to be the masters in South Africa because of the colour of their skin. I grew up in apartheid South Africa, where the whites had a terrific life and simply ignored the astonishing suffering that was going on around them, which is a sort of guilt I had to deal with when I came here. Nelson Mandela was in prison on Robben Island, which you can see from the pretty white beaches of Sea Point where my family and I used to laze in the sun – you could see the Island but you didn't see it, you didn't think about what was going on there.

Being Jewish, do you think you were kinder?

No, being honest. I wish I could answer yes, and there is a small but honourable roll-call of Jewish South Africans who did make the connection and really fought the system; they are heroic figures to me, but I'm afraid my family were simply middle-of-the-road people just wanting a good life.

Early on in life, you were torn between art and theatre, or specifically between Mac and Esther.

Yes. I was very ill-fitting in the society I was growing up in; white South African society was very macho, very sports-oriented, very extrovert, and I was a small, weedy chap, not at all good at games. Drawing and painting became my saviour; a very charismatic teacher at school called Mac saw some talent and really made me a favourite, and best of all he got me out of PT! But I was already a very shy kid and the drawing was making me more introverted, so my parents sent me to what was called elocution, which was a more respectable term than acting. But it was acting, and led by an outrageous figure called Esther Caplan, who I describe in the book as Sybil Thorndike with a touch of Ethel Merman thrown in – very theatrical, very warm, and the great thing about her was that she was interested in modern theatre, so although we weren't seeing the plays of Pinter and Wesker, she would always get copies of them to read. I had quite a progressive early training.

It's clear that you knew you were gay from very early on, but those feelings were simply not allowed in South Africa and in fact had only just been legalised in England when you arrived here; that must have presented a very difficult childhood for you?

Yes, I felt I was a Martian landed on earth. All my instincts were towards my own sex but it didn't seem to be something that anybody else in the country was doing. It was the first of my identities that I locked away and tried not to be; later, when I came to England, I would try not to be white South African; as I went into acting, I would pretend not to be Jewish because I couldn't see many examples of Jewish actors getting classical parts. I ended up locking away all these different identities which of course is nonsense because you end up being nobody. Later, my life resounded to the swoosh and bang of closet doors opening and this book, in a way, is the final coming out of everything else as well.

Much to everybody's astonishment, you were rejected by two main drama schools.

Yes, it was a real shock to be turned down. We'd found out that the two top drama schools were Central and RADA; I auditioned at the first just a few days after arriving in England and at that time we were so confident that we'd even got a bed-sit in Swiss Cottage – we were that stupid about it. The audition was over in seconds; a group of us were sitting waiting and the registrar put her head round the door and said 'Sorry, none of you today.' It was that simple and I'd travelled half way round the world. Then I went to RADA and a few days later a letter arrived saying that not only had I failed the audition and they didn't wish me to try again, but that they strongly urged me to think about a different career. Then my parents had to go back to South Africa, and it was alarming – London was a big, baffling city if you'd been brought up in Cape Town. But eventually, when I got to drama school at Webber-Douglas, I started to enjoy it.

You talk about acting in the shadow of Olivier, purely because of some of the parts that have presented themselves to you; the creation of Richard III must have been doubly difficult for you, partly because you wanted to create your own portrayal, but also because you decided to play him on crutches.

It was a dangerous thing, and I remember lots of discussion about whether it was right because sometimes the best ideas are dangerously close to the worst ideas. The idea actually came from an Achilles tendon accident I'd had, when I'd lived on crutches for about six weeks; when I started to research Richard III in different ways, one of them was to visit homes for the disabled to work out which condition Richard might have, and of course I started seeing lots of people on crutches. In discussions with the director and designer, the idea started to grow because crutches give an almost four-legged look, and Richard is always abused with animal imagery. We proceeded slowly, but you could feel it start to become exciting, the potential of this very disabled man who could nevertheless cross the stage in about two bounds and in fact move faster than anyone else at court. Crutches are very useful as weapons, and they're rather phallic instruments, so eventually we did go with it and it proved to be quite successful.

Your father's death affected you very deeply; after it had happened, you sat down and wrote a long letter to him and you say that there was a sea-change in your feelings once you'd said all the things you wanted to say – suddenly life became a better place to be.

Ironically, the last time I was on this stage was playing Cyrano in an RSC production. By the time I came to do that part, I'd become very interested in emotional recall in acting and I felt that Cyrano in particular needed that; the incredible love that he has with Roxanne – the actor really has to play that with great emotional commitment and re-find it night after night. The great balcony scene – where Roxanne thinks she's talking to Christian, the handsome young man that she's attracted to, but in fact it's Cyrano who can never declare his own love – is a very wonderful and poignant scene, so I used to sit in the wings beforehand, searching for emotional recall; curiously I couldn't find it in the actual experiences of my own life when I'd been hopelessly in love or infatuated; my great case of unrequited love, in a way, was Dad in that he and I didn't really have much of a relationship, and because he had died by then I found that I could summon up images of him that would move me in just the right way and I'd come on stage and play the scene; when it worked it was wonderful and the scene felt really very honest. We played the show for about six months, but it became harder and harder to freshen up that sensation and there was eventually a performance where the images of him failed to trigger the right responses in me, and I went back to the hotel and really finally got off my chest so much about him and us. It did help, but in a way it can never be fully resolved, a relationship like that when a person has died, because the thing that I can never do is simply hug him, hold him – that is obviously something I will now never do.

From a wonderful range of parts, one that stands out for me because you so clearly enjoyed being him is the painter Stanley Spencer; is it the actor and the painter in you that made this role so successful?

Yes. With most parts you find there's something you have to learn to do on stage that's not natural to you; for Cyrano, I had to learn to sword-fight and the wimp in me was always saying 'ouch' even though I'd trained for months; when those moments come up in the show you just grit your teeth and get through them. But suddenly here was a part where I had to be seen sketching and it was just wonderful to be able to do that without thinking because drawing is the most natural thing to me – I've been doing it since I was four. There was something about that that led me to the character; I can be a terrible procrastinator as an actor, imagining all sorts of problems, but somehow with Stanley Spencer I just went straight to him. He fascinates me because he was so honest with himself – quite monstrous in a way and completely ego-centric, and yet he was honest about that and in his paintings, too; they're his view of the world and he doesn't care, he just has to put it down on canvas, whether it's those startlingly frank portraits

of himself and his second wife, Patricia, or those glorious biblical scenes where Christ is carrying the cross down Cookham High Street. It's such a singular view of the world, and I really loved him and loved playing him.

We journey through your anxieties of not quite getting the awards you were hoping to get; of course, they did start to come in and then you received a knighthood – what did that mean to you?

Well, it happened in such a strange way and it's typical of my life that fantastic things sometimes come quite close to disastrous things, the two things just narrowly miss one another or even collide. Greg, my partner, and I had just finished a run of *Macbeth* in America and a pile of correspondence had built up while we were away. Greg happened to be passing through the room and picked up one envelope that looked rather important; I opened it and – according to Greg – staggered backwards and went white because it was a knighthood. It was ten o'clock in the morning and we had some champagne in the fridge, so we were about to open it when Greg said you really must go and phone your mother to tell her; my mother has always been a very ambitious woman for me and Greg – as the dutiful son-in-law – knew she had to know first. You could hear her cheer across the world without the telephone. I was just going back upstairs for the champagne when I started to think that something was a little bit odd because the letter was from the Foreign Office and it referred to an honorary knighthood. I phoned and asked what that meant, and was told it was because I was South African. I explained that I wasn't, that I was born there but had been naturalised since 1979, and a voice at the other end said 'Really? Oh dear, oh dear – red faces all round then.' He told me it was therefore in the gift of another department and I'd better just forget that the letter ever arrived. Of course, I then had to phone my mother back to tell her the knighthood was off. She was devastated. Luckily, with admirable speed, another letter arrived, this time from the Cabinet Office to apologise and say that I was now a knight, and an ordinary knight. I rang my mother and said the knighthood was back on and she said 'Are you sure because I don't think I can take much more of this!'. But she was able to come over and come to Buckingham Palace with my brother and sister, and it was a great day.

Susannah York

Amy's View
by David Hare
May, 2001

The Loves of Shakespeare's Women
February, 2002

You have some wonderful film credits to your career, and *The Killing of Sister George* was groundbreaking at the time – did you enjoy making it?

Yes, I did. Robert Aldrich was a terrific director – huge and avuncular and massive; he just made things fun. And Beryl I loved. Actually, I got on terribly well with both my ladies, Coral and Beryl, but they were chalk and cheese and I often felt like the jam in the middle; Coral was quite waspish about Beryl, and Beryl was sometimes downright rude about Coral, but there was a healthy respect between them. It was a happy film to make.

You played Sir Thomas More's daughter in *A Man For All Seasons*, and that stands out, too, for the excellence of the film-making.

Fred Zinnemann certainly knew how to do things, and he chose the best – costumes, sets, actors and, of course, a wonderful story to tell: the film was based on that old adage, 'the play's the thing'. Another director who did that was Tony Richardson with *Tom Jones*, which was a much looser structure but again started out from a great novel, then added John Osborne's script and the cream of actors – Edith Evans, Joan Greenwood, Hugh Griffiths, Wilfred Lawson; all fabulous people. When we're good, we're very good, the Brits, but there's the other corollary, too.

Is theatre your great love?

That's where I started and doubtless that's where I'll end. I love the theatre, but I enjoy film too, and if I do one for too long I miss the other. The wonderful thing about theatre is

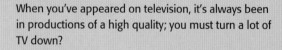

that you're there from A to Z; it's you up there, and you're pitched in. Film is a director's medium: you're in his hands, and it's up to him if he cuts to you or if you end up on the cutting-room floor. It's strange that you get wonderful theatre actors for whom it just doesn't work on film – Laurence Olivier, for example – or wonderful film actresses like Marilyn Monroe who don't have the machinery or even the wish for the stage. I'm lucky that I can play in both fields. At first, I wanted only the stage, and it was quite a surprise to me to be wanted for film; I was quite snobbish for a while, thinking that film was for pretty people; little did I know how hard it really is and what discipline it requires. So it's been a humbling experience, film, and I've always got something out of it – even the bum ones! You don't flash the titles around, but there have been a few of those. And there have been times when I've been guilty of not doing my homework; certain scripts I've looked at and thought I could make a silk purse out of a sow's ear, but it hasn't worked like that because, with film, the all is in the direction.

When you've appeared on television, it's always been in productions of a high quality; you must turn a lot of TV down?

Oh no, I don't. With TV, you're fashionable or you're not and the truth of the matter is I'm not fashionable at the moment. To be brutally frank, I would love to do some good television and my agent is very good and diligent in putting me up for things, but they say too old, too young, too this, too that – that's just the way it is. It's true that turning up on quiz shows just to be on television doesn't appeal – but I know I wouldn't be any good at them, so there's no point in my doing them! One life's all you've got, so you want to do the things you're better at.

Who are your favourite leading men?

I've worked with some wonderful ones – Albert Finney, Peter O'Toole, Montgomery Clift, Marlon Brando, Paul Schofield; I could go on, as I could about the women – Elizabeth Taylor, Beryl, Jane Fonda. Elizabeth Taylor was funny, warm, generous – she had her own kind of insecurities, but she was immensely attractive. Something I've found in this business is that people who are good at their job are marvellous people – they have a generosity of soul.

You're known for having a very distinctive voice, as well…

It's only in more recent stages of my career that people have started to pick up on the voice – I suppose that's because other things are starting to go a bit! But it's been a surprise to me. When I did my first audition at RADA, rushing around tearing passion to tatters on the stage, the principal said to me 'It's very fortunate that we've had six St. Joans already this morning so we knew what you were talking about'. There was never any problem with the level of the voice, but I did have to learn technique for most things and particularly to speak clearly.

Your latest stage role is in a one-woman show, *The Loves of Shakespeare's Women*; how did that come about?

Devising a one-woman show is very ambitious. I was looking for a theme, and originally started with the idea of doing an Ages of Woman like *The Seven Ages of Man*, with a variety of women from youth to old age. But I needed something to thread them onto one necklace and, as I collected Shakespeare's characters, I realised the theme of love ran through all of them: romantic love; family love; love of power; love of God, mercy and truth in every aspect.

What Shakespeare roles have you particularly enjoyed in the past?

Well, at RADA I played Rosalind, Juliet, Beatrice and Ophelia. At school, I remember being heartbroken not to be cast as Shylock, but I did play Puck and that was a real kicking off point for me. This new show talks a lot about role swapping, gender and cross-dressing, a device which Shakespeare uses so often, always for protection or enablement. You can't help feeling that he's expressing his feelings about a woman's position in his world: that to be safe or to be heeded, that's what a woman had to do – you had to be a man to be a woman.

Is it nice to be back in Cambridge, because you're no stranger to the city, are you?

I lived in Newnham for two years and I come back regularly because I've still got friends here. I loved it, but I found it utterly impossible to be a working mother, taking the children to school then driving straight to London to work, so in the end I moved back down. But the air and the greenery – I love it here.

Prunella Scales

The Cherry Orchard
by Anton Chekhov
May, 2000
The External
by Rodney Clark
May, 2001

Prunella Scales – that's a wonderful name for an actress; is it the one you were born with?

No, it was my mother's maiden name. My father's name was 'Illingworth', but I thought Prunella Illingworth was a bit long and I might not get any billing, and as my mother had been an actress it seemed appropriate. My father was a sales rep, but he loved the theatre and did work with local amateurs, so I had a lot of encouragement from both of them.

You've trained in both London and New York – what was the contrast there?

I was lucky enough to train at the very short-lived London Old Vic Theatre School with Michel St. Denis, George Devine and Glenn Byam Shaw. It only ran for five years and was closed to run the Old Vic Theatre, which then re-opened – so there aren't many of us left. I went there when I was just seventeen, and I had plaits and very thick glasses and was rather studious – I don't think any of the staff thought I was very attractive and I had rather a tough time there. To everybody's intense surprise, I did get a job at the end of the training, and I went to the Bristol Old Vic in a production of *The Matchmaker*, directed by Tyrone Guthrie, which transferred to New York. I wanted to see the city, but it was only a small part that I had and I was going out of my mind with boredom during the day. Then a friend of mine told me to 'go to class'; I'd heard that Lee Strasberg wasn't appropriate for English work – which is nonsense because Strasberg and Method is very interesting – so I went to the Berghoff Studio and studied with Uta Hagen, who became and still is my guru. She's eighty now, but still a wonderful

teacher and actress. Her greatest success over here was in *Who's Afraid of Virginia Woolf?*, and for her eightieth birthday celebrations they did a reading with Jonathan Pryce and Mia Farrow as the juvenile – it's extraordinary that an actress of eighty can look and sound forty plus and be completely convincing. So I went to class there every week for the five months I was in New York, and it changed my life and blew my mind completely.

You've appeared in so many classic plays and films, but one of the things you'll always be remembered for – whether you like it or not – is *Fawlty Towers*. In that you became a household name overnight; how did it come about?

I had done various television – *Marriage Lines* with Richard Briers, for example – so that was fortunate, because if you're connected with a popular television series you do get more work in the theatre, and I love the nature of English acting because you can work in all media and they feed each other. For *Fawlty Towers*, we did a pilot, and the then Head of Comedy at the BBC was walking up and down the corridor saying 'I don't know what John's thinking about – he's gone mad'. But they decided to make the first six, and they were incredibly successful so we did another six, then John and Connie decided they didn't want to do any more, so we stopped – and I think quite rightly, because they were exquisitely written with enormous discipline and rigour. If you didn't know it by Wednesday morning, then watch out – and we all appreciated that because the speed was incomparable; nothing's ever been played faster, and the assurance of it was wonderful. Looking at it twenty-something years on, it still seems fast, unlike many other comedies of the time; it's as tight as ever and very impressive, and I'm extremely proud and grateful to have been associated with it.

Mapp and Lucia was another wonderful series – did you enjoy that?

Enormously. It was a very happy job and I wish we could have done more. We filmed it in Rye, and I had the padding and the 1920s and 30s costumes; we'd film a scene going up the high street with a shopping basket and I'd think it was so over the top, that dreadful waddle – then as soon as the director said 'cut', doors all the way down the street would open and fourteen shoppers would walk back up in exactly the same way because the cobbles made you do it. I went into the dressmaker's there one day in my costume, and nobody turned a hair! They thought I was a customer from next door.

As far as you're concerned, it's a house full of thespians – do you discuss work when you get home?

Oh yes. Tim's seen this production three times and he produces a sheaf of notes, and I do the same for him. It's invaluable. The same is true of the kids, even our youngest son, who's not an actor. Tim and I always discuss what work we will and won't do, and I ask his advice on everything.

I believe when you're not working you both like to take to the river?

Yes, we have a narrow-boat with a permanent mooring at Newbury, but we've been up and down the country on her. At the moment, we can't use her because our son, Samuel, is living on her in Stratford while he's playing Richard II – he's got a lovely mooring, just opposite the Dirty Duck. We've lived on her when we've been working in Bristol or in Leeds, and we've called her after our accountant because our accountant is the only reason we can afford her!

Do you have problems going shopping now because you're so well known in a certain supermarket?

Well, I certainly shop there myself but people don't recognise me without the specs and the wig. When people do come up to me in the street, they say 'Haven't you got thin? Are you all right?'. I'm very grateful to it – I think the ads are beautifully written and I won't say anything I don't believe to be true. Tesco have a very good record: they're increasingly buying British and organic, and Tesco Metros keep inner cities alive after dark in a very positive way. And of course it helps to finance my theatre work, because subsidised regional touring isn't very well funded.

Timothy West

The External
by Rodney Clark
May, 2001

King Lear
by William Shakespeare
November, 2002

Even a distinguished actor like Timothy West had parents who wanted him to have a 'proper job' rather than follow in their theatrical footsteps. Settling at first for selling office furniture, West then became a sound recordist for EMI before his spare time eventually took him further and further away from such notions of a conventional career. 'By that time, I was a member of so many amateur dramatic societies that it really seemed sensible to be paid for the thing to which I was devoting most of my time and energy,' he laughs. In those flourishing days of the repertory company, a full grounding in all things theatrical was much easier to come by and, like many great performers, he started out as an Assistant Stage Manager; it's something he's never likely to forget, and he recalls here what a typical week involved:

'On Sunday nights, I helped with the fit-up, placed the furniture, decorated the set and made the tea. On Monday morning, I would return any items borrowed from last week, then walk the set for the electricians to focus the lamps; I'd clear up and sweep the stage before going to the railway station to pick up the wigs and costumes for the afternoon's dress rehearsal, at which I would operate the sound system, arrange the props and handle all the changes in the interval. If I was also in the play, which was often the case, my performance somehow had to be fitted in with the rest of these other duties. That evening, the same routine had to be gone through again in front of the public.

'On Tuesday morning at the first blocking rehearsal for the next play, I would mark out on stage the outlines of the set. I may have been playing a part in this, too. A production meeting followed, in which a list was given to me of furniture and properties which had to be obtained from the store or hired from local shops or, as a last resort, constructed by me.

I would start this on Tuesday afternoon. On Tuesday evening, another performance, of course. On Wednesday morning, there'd be a rehearsal of next week's Act One, then a matinee and then an evening show. Act Two would be rehearsed on Thursday morning and, by this time, the scenic artist would be needing my assistance in the paint shop.

'On Friday afternoon, having rehearsed Act Three in the morning, we would do a complete run-through with the new furniture, and there would be a rush to store this and re-set for the evening performance. Saturday consisted of a final run-through, a matinee and the final evening performance of the present play; after this, we would strike the set, store the scenery and carefully wrap up anything we had hired or borrowed ready for return on Monday, and perhaps get away by 2am on Sunday morning. On Sunday evening, we started all over again.'

One imagines that things are a little easier these days, but it seems a terrible shame that today's young actors no longer have the benefit of the all-round training that rep offered. West agrees: 'It was an inevitable tragedy that rep would collapse when television became a general audience resource. Some of it was a bit crummy and couldn't compete because of the time-scale we had to work with but nevertheless, the fact that you were exposed to an incredible number of different authors' work, different styles and different forms of production is something that is absolutely unavailable today. Even the most adventurous drama school which packs its curriculum with actual

performances can't give you at the end of a year a taste of Shakespeare, Shaw, Wilde, Chekhov, Ibsen, Pinero, Coward, Moliére, Agatha Christie and anybody else you can name.'

Weekly rep wasn't the only institution that West encountered during his early career: the various digs that he stayed in were a constant source of entertainment. The world of the theatrical landlady becomes almost a play within a play as he recalls some of the pinafored treasures he has known: 'In Salisbury at the beginning of my career, you had to pay an extra two shillings for a hot bath on top of the room charge. The way the landlady arranged to get the money was to unscrew the hot tap and replace it on prior payment of the two shillings. Well, one Saturday night when I was still working as an ASM, I returned to my digs very late and very dirty. I couldn't possibly go to bed in her sheets in that state, but neither did I want to wake her at that hour, so ingeniously I took a pocket pen knife, unscrewed the top of the cold tap, fixed it on to the hot tap and ran myself a bath. No sooner had I got into it than the door was flung open and this irate woman in curl papers demanded her two shillings. I explained that, dressed as I was, it was unlikely that I had the money about me, but she marched me down the corridor to my room and made me get it out of my trouser pocket before she'd go away and allow me to enjoy my bath. I moved out the next morning.'

Then, of course, there was Mrs Alma McKay. West lapses into a broad Yorkshire accent as he describes possibly the most famous of all theatrical landladies. 'She lived at Astra House, "home of the stars", at 10 Daisy Avenue, Manchester and she was a terrific Mrs Malaprop: if she could get a word wrong, she would. She'd say "I've got somebody coming to see me from the *Sunday Times* to ask me about the time I was the first person in Manchester to clap eyes on the Deep Sea Rolls". I'd been imagining bread rolls with a prawn hanging limply out of them, but no – it really was the Dead Sea Scrolls in the hands of an Egyptian archaeologist who'd come to stay.'

West is renowned for his work with Prospect Theatre Company, but his time there was in some ways the result of an unhappy experience with the RSC, during which a habit of trawling through wastepaper baskets had unforeseen consequences: 'Three of us had a spy ring and we put a long gap in a play to good use by going up to the offices. In those days, the secretaries all used Gestetner machines; when they'd copied what they were doing, the original stencil was screwed up and put in the wastepaper bin but you could still read it, so we used to go up and retrieve those stencils, iron them out and see what was going on – who was going to be engaged to play what, what they were getting paid and all the inter-departmental business. This was all very interesting, but on one occasion it proved to be very, very depressing. I found a typed table which divided the present company into five categories, with A being the obvious stars of the season, E being the walk-ons and the others graded in between. I fully expected to be, if not a B, then most certainly a C, and I found I was in the D list. I just sat there and sobbed – it was like a Woody Allen movie. I was destroyed by it and decided to leave the company. I think these things happen for the best, and I moved on to Prospect Theatre Company, with whom I had an almost permanent relationship for sixteen years. But that was the end of my going through wastepaper bins.'

The title of West's biography, *A Moment Towards the End of the Play,* is drawn from the way in which the magazine *Theatre World* captioned some of its photographs, but it also sounds a warning note. 'It reflects my belief that we are perhaps nearing the end of the period of what we have always recognised as "a play": the single play has given way to the series; the dialogue film about human relations has given way to the special effects blockbuster; and in the West End there are considerably more musicals than straight plays: I don't think this signals the doom of the play, but I do think it's a warning.'

Fenella Fielding

Lady Windermere's Fan
by Oscar Wilde
April, 2001

Fenella Fielding, Christopher Biggins and Mandy Morton take tea...

MANDY: Let's get this tea party underway... here comes the tea.

CHRISTOPHER: Garibaldis, I hope.

MANDY: Garibaldis and ginger nuts.

FENELLA: This is very Oscar Wilde. You know they did a survey of which biscuits you should feel least guilty about eating and one of them was garibaldi because some of the stuff that's very bad for you is displaced by many, many raisins; they got five stars and ginger nuts, which get my vote, got three but I can't remember why.

CHRISTOPHER: Would you mind if I asked Miss Fielding a very personal question? Fenella – do you dunk?!

FENELLA: Whenever possible!

CHRISTOPHER: She looks like a dunker, doesn't she?

FENELLA: He's got this terrible confession out of me without even trying!

CHRISTOPHER: It's wonderful to be back in Cambridge again, and we're having a really good time. It's nice to be doing an Oscar Wilde play which was written in 1896 but which still stands up today; audiences really laugh and are intrigued – it's fabulous stuff. Fenella and I are playing brother and sister in this – we were cast because we're so alike!

FENELLA: Same size and height, and such wonderful legs…

CHRISTOPHER: But I've often said that it's very like *OK!* and *Hello* magazines: it's all gossip, everybody talking about each other in a very nice way, nothing really malicious, people having relationships with mistresses– it's exactly what's happening today. Nothing's changed.

FENELLA: Except back then people were much more judgemental. You could do what you liked as long as you didn't get found out, and that applies today, too, although not in quite the same way.

MANDY: Fenella – this can't be your first visit to Cambridge?

FENELLA: No, I did *Gigi* here, and I think I did *The Ghost Train* – a revival, I hasten to add! But I also had one of my very early jobs here in panto with Danny Kaye.

MANDY: People will instantly place you in the *Carry On* films and those marvellous *Doctor* programmes.

FENELLA: Yes, you're absolutely right and it was with the cream of comic talent, people like Leslie Phillips and Hattie Jacques.

MANDY: She's one of my favourite actresses – what was she like?

FENELLA: I was terrified of her. I only ever met her in the make-up room and I just kept very quiet.

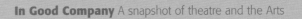

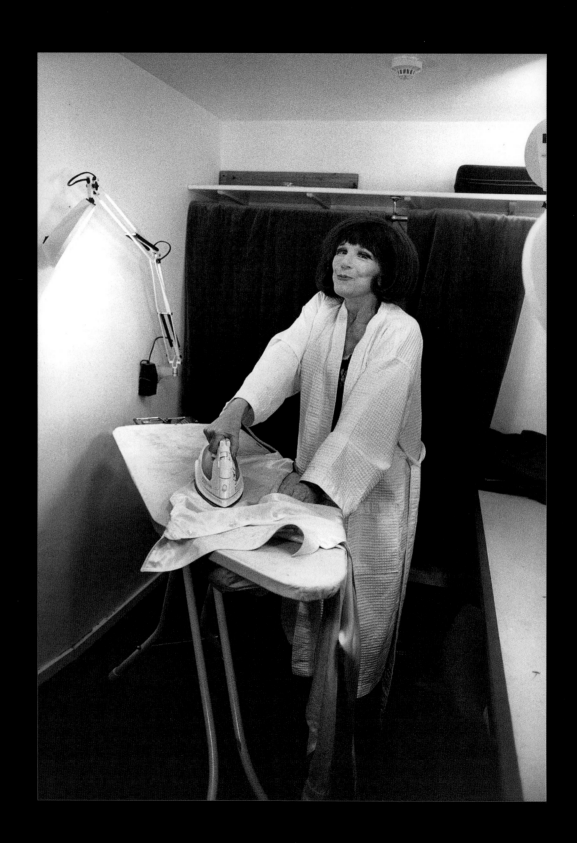

CHRISTOPHER: I worked with her in a recording of a children's show, *The Owl and the Pussycat Went to See…*; she played the Pussycat, and it was towards the end of her career. She was entrancing, and if you listen to it now she sounds so young.

FENELLA: She had terrific sex appeal. When I was little, an uncle of mine took me along to The Players and I didn't realise until a couple of years later that he was absolutely besotted with her. She was jolly pretty, and had this amazing way of turning her eyes — it was like an electric jolt through the whole theatre. Amazing.

MANDY: Going back to the *Carry Ons*, that must have been the most amazing time to be in films and you were a bit of a sex symbol yourself.

FENELLA: You know, I didn't do anything vampy in *Carry on Screaming…*

MANDY: But everybody remembers you that way.

FENELLA: That's the amazing thing, but I played it completely straight like the Fairy Princess.

MANDY: Comedy's very important to both of you, isn't it?

CHRISTOPHER: Yes, and there's a big difference between comedians and comic actors; Ronnie Barker is a great comic actor, Ronnie Corbett is a comedian, and it's fascinating. I agree with you that Fenella is a great comic actor.

MANDY: She radiates it without doing too much.

CHRISTOPHER: Absolutely, and that's the secret of it all.

FENELLA: I was once asked in a very intense interview if I could say that anyone was a great inspiration and I just couldn't think of anybody. That would have sounded terribly vain, and I suddenly remembered seeing a dog act at the Palladium called Neno the Wonderdog and it was incredible. So I told the interviewer all about this, about dogs who jumped around and sat on stools, and about the moment when the star, Neno the Wonderdog, bounced on and looked at the gallery, smiled at the audience. So I watched what Neno did, and I loved the way he took his calls: he ran on, sat in the centre and raised a paw, then ran back on a little ball…

CHRISTOPHER: Star quality!

FENELLA: I suddenly thought, I don't know where I'm going with this but if one day I'm able to walk on a stage and, without doing anything in particular, the audience knows what I mean I shall begin to think I'm getting somewhere.

CHRISTOPHER: And I love it during the *Lady Windermere* curtain call when she comes on on that ball!

MANDY: Christopher collects art – do you collect anything?

FENELLA: Well, it's extraordinary because just recently somebody rang up and said we understand you collect clocks; I told him that I didn't but he was insistent, so I asked him to hang on while I went to have a look – and he was absolutely right: I am potty about clock and watch faces.

MANDY: Who have you enjoyed working with?

CHRISTOPHER: It's hard because it's a bit like going back to the last thing you did, but I loved working with Donny Osmond last year; he was enchanting, the most lovely man with a great sense of humour. For him to hold my hand and sing to me was one of the great moments of my career! By the same token, I've enjoyed meeting people I haven't had the chance to work with like Frank Sinatra, which was a great thrill.

FENELLA: It is terribly hard to say, but I did enjoy acting with Ian McKellen when I did *Hedda Gabler;* anybody who plays that part regards it as their own from then on and no one else must play it. I did a really marvellous Henry James play with Edward Woodward, and that was a meeting of minds, too, a lovely thing to do.

MANDY: Are you what you would regard as a theatre actress?

FENELLA: Well, that's where you hone and polish this, that and the other, and you learn how to condense it for other media. If you've started in the theatre, which I did, and even if you do lots of film, every now and again you must go back to theatre to make sure you're doing things right. There, you have to give an audience the confidence to respond in the way you would like them to; people aren't always sure of themselves – and why should they be? – so, whether you want them to laugh or to listen intently, you have to get the message over.

Anna Carteret

Copenhagen
by Michael Frayn
September, 2001

'Copenhagen is Michael Frayn's own idea of what happened at that mysterious meeting between Werner Heisenberg and Niels Bohr in 1941; it's not the true interpretation, but dramatically it's very interesting because out of it comes the whole question of responsibility for building the atom bomb: there's the moral element and the philosophical angle, and it's a fascinating play at all levels.

'For an actor, it's incredibly intense because we're on stage throughout so we really have to listen to each other as we go through the various phases of the play. And it's been an incredibly steep learning curve: I left school at fifteen and I never even did physics or chemistry, so I had no idea what these things meant; it's been like an adult education course for me within three weeks of rehearsal. I'm still learning on stage: it couldn't be more different to *Juliet Bravo!*'

Jane Montgomery and the Cambridge Greek Play

Electra
by Sophocles
October, 2001

Aside from interruptions during wartime, the triennial Greek Play has been a Cambridge tradition since 1882. Staged first at the Theatre Royal and then at the New Theatre, the Greek Play moved to the Arts at the earliest opportunity and was part of the opening season in 1936; that first production was *The Frogs* of Aristophanes, directed by Provost Sheppard and George Rylands, with music by Walter Leigh. Performed as always in the original Greek, *The Frogs* proved so popular that the four matinees originally advertised were sold out in time for an extra one to be announced, which also produced a capacity house. School parties from all over the country travelled to Cambridge to see the play, and meticulous arrangements had to be made for accommodation, meals and visits to Cambridge colleges.

Back then, Greek plays were viewed by many as a bold experiment; nevertheless, the Cambridge Greek Play attracted a wide audience, with special trains bringing crowds from London and productions reviewed enthusiastically by the national press. Some of this popularity stemmed from the fact that acclaimed composers such as Stanford, Parry and Vaughan-Williams had been persuaded to write original music for the productions, but the biggest draw was the power, the universal quality of the drama being played out on stage. In the 21st century, very little has changed: when the 2001 *Electra* opened at the Arts – complete with English surtitles for the very first time – the raw, emotional impact of the play and the hypnotic appeal of the language led once more to a packed house for every performance.

'Once you've read *Electra* – and especially once you've seen a good production – you'll find other plays just slightly lacking. *Hamlet* will still be brilliant, but long-winded compared to Sophocles' hour and a half of perfectly-chiselled theatricality; *Hedda* will remain a magnificent monster, but bland when compared to the staggering peaks and troughs of Electra's character. There'll be other plays that move and shock you, other plays that make you leave the theatre with jellied legs, but it will be hard to find one that can ever be as all-consumingly, heart-rendingly beautiful in its despair, or as coruscating in its truthfulness.

'I speak from experience. Eighteen years ago, I read *Electra* for the first time. Imagine the scene: the mid-eighties; shaggy perms and pictures of Andrew Ridgeley torn from *Smash Hits;* fifteen pubescent school girls in a terrapin hut with a leak, trudging through Greek Literature in Translation 'O' Level. We had a wonderful teacher but, to be honest, we were all a bit bored; January was bleak and lunch time a double period away. Then we started to read our new set text. I can still remember the white-hot ball of adrenaline that came thundering into my belly as we read. My world was completely transformed in the space of just half an hour, and my reaction was not unique: the whole class became caught up in the drama. We were transformed from time-serving school girls to Greek tragedy converts, loving this play and debating passionately the rights and wrongs of Electra's predicament.

'*Electra* has a strange and haunting potency. It's a work of theatrical brilliance, faultlessly structured and relentlessly paced; it's a thriller, and the story of Orestes, exiled young prince returning home to exact vengeance for his murdered father, is the sort of rite of passage you find in the best Westerns and darkest gangster movies. But the added ingredient is that revenge involves matricide: to avenge the father, he must slaughter the mother. Moreover Sophocles brilliantly avoids creating an obvious drama about the justice of slaughter by leaving us to watch – with fascinated horror – the central figure of Electra, the degraded but defiant daughter who has stayed behind to be the thorn in her murderous mother's flesh. There are no rights or wrongs in this play, no black and white – just a nihilistic vision of a world where fundamentalism rules and ancient, internecine feuds are passed down from generation to generation. Families collapse, friends become enemies, and justice excuses atrocity.'

Jane Montgomery

April de Angelis

She Stoops to Conquer and
A Laughing Matter
January 2003

A *Laughing Matter* runs in rep with *She Stoops to Conquer* – what's the premise behind that and the play in general?

Out of Joint wanted me to write a contemporary play to run alongside a new 18th century play that hadn't been done before, but we couldn't find one. We read loads and they were all so horribly bad that we ended up deciding that *She Stoops to Conquer* was just so fantastic that we shouldn't go any further. There's a whole story behind that play of it not being put on by Garrick at Drury Lane because it was considered too low and therefore too incendiary; he thought it would cause a riot or disgrace because of its vulgarity and because it had too much laughter in it. I was investigating Garrick, and found that there was also a rumour of an illegitimate son who was a young actor in his company. That was the starting point for drawing those two strands together, and that's the premise of the play: Garrick has to decide whether to maintain respectability by staging a lesser play by a dull clergymen, or to choose Goldsmith's work and risk his reputation; the son likes Goldsmith's play and in a way they're connected – Garrick turns both of them down. After *She Stoops to Conquer* and Sheridan's work, theatre died for a hundred years in terms of great plays; it wasn't just Garrick's fault – he loved the theatre, but he saved it in one way and destroyed it in another.

You couldn't ask for a better line-up than characters like Goldsmith, Garrick and Johnson, with cameos for Reynolds, Burke and Boswell, and you must have enjoyed creating them, but how much licence did you take?

I did enjoy it, but there was so much reading. I've taken a fair bit of licence, but nothing is completely out of the bounds of possibility: they did really meet in a club called The Turk's Head, and they met to combat Johnson's depression. The 18th century's mad on conversation – they had nothing else, in a way, so they were always discussing things, and the relationships between them are real. Some of the things they say have been recorded by Boswell in his life of Johnson, and others are things Johnson might have said. So the heart of it is all true, but because it's a play you have to take licence, otherwise you'd just be putting slabs of history on the stage that nobody would want to watch.

There's a fantastic sense of what Drury Lane must have been like at the time, too.

Yes, the company and I were really shocked by the thought of the riots that went on in theatres. Audiences were really badly behaved: they threw people over the side; they stormed the stage; if they didn't like something, they'd tear the theatre apart. There was real audience power – these days, we're so used to audiences sitting there clapping politely. Poor Garrick – they made him come out and get on his knees at one point, and he had to plead with them. And backstage in a theatre is a wonderful lively world – and then probably more than now.

Something Out of Joint does particularly well is to throw two periods of time together and see what they say about each other. *She Stoops to Conquer* **was a watershed moment in terms of its antithesis to sentimental comedy – is now a moment of change?**

I think it's hard to draw parallels because we're very used to wild comedy now. We've got a real appetite for comedy and we're not afraid of it, but what is similar is this idea of spin where you have to pretend to be something in order to please and placate and manipulate people. As for theatre itself, writers have always struggled to get their work on and it's still like that now.

Nick Moran

Four Knights in Knaresborough
by Paul Webb
October, 2001

After the success of *Lock, Stock and Two Smoking Barrels*, do you think that the fact you're now starring in a play will help to get younger audiences into the theatres?

I have trouble getting used to the idea that the people promoting the show would use me to sell it, but I want to make sure I do everything I can to make sure people come and see it. It's definitely a good time to be appealing to younger audiences, to say 'this theatre is yours – take it and enjoy it'. There's a running gag with the cast that I'm too big a star to be lost in Wolverhampton, trying to work out where the car park is but, if you get caught up with the Hollywood stuff, you lose your sense of where you're going. I don't mind why they end up coming to the show as long as they do – it's a really class bit of theatre.

Is it the stage you want to concentrate on for a while?

I'm trying to do a bit of everything at the moment, switching between plays and films, and I'm really enjoying that.

Do you do lots of research for a role like this?

I'm an advocate of idleness, to a certain extent, in as much as I think the hard work has been done by the writer because he's sat down and thought for ages and thought really long and hard before he wrote anything. It's such a doss job being an actor, because it's all done for you and all you've got to do is make the brilliance of other people look good – that's what you do, essentially. I think Paul [Webb] has done a really good job with the play and it's actually all in there.

So you can wrap yourself up in knots doing all sorts of silly anal research which is irrelevant, but it tends to be just a means of warding off the evil spirits of self consciousness. If you spent as much time researching the bit of paper that you're reading as opposed to some load of old slightly irrelevant material on the internet…there isn't enough time to research the script, let alone look into irrelevancies. So you mustn't get side-tracked by that. That's my note to all you students.

Stephanie Cole

So Long Life
by Peter Nichols
October 2001

Albert Finney came to see *A Passionate Woman* when we were in Guildford. He came backstage to talk to me afterwards, and was utterly enchanting. We talked for about half an hour about acting and the theatre. He is completely passionate about the business and unaffected by his own celebrity. Then he said something, and it seems silly when you think that I'd been in the business about thirty-six years when he said this, but it was one of the best bits of advice anybody's ever given me. It wasn't really offered as advice, we were just talking about acting, and he said, 'I sometimes think of acting as like being a jazz musician.'

'How so?'

'Well, you know how to play your instrument superbly, you know what the music is, and when you get to actually perform, you just get out there and – you just blow dat sax.'

He sent me a first-night card for the West End run saying, 'Dear Steph, Get out there and blow dat sax. Love, Albie.'

If I hadn't been an actor, I might have wanted to be a philologist, a linguistics expert. Words are very subtle. You can have a line of script, and you know what the character is trying to say, but there is one word in that line – and it could be an 'and' instead of an 'if' or a 'but' – which, because English is probably one of the most subtle languages in the world, will alter the whole nuance of the sentence. I love that; it gives me such pleasure. That is one of the reasons I love poetry so much – because of the importance of the exact choice of words.

In real life we talk in clichés much of the time, but when you hear a cliché in theatre or television drama or in the cinema, it is quite ludicrous. This is why I get so irritated when people admire Agatha Christie's plays so much, because frankly she was a sublimely bad writer of dialogue.

Although, having said that, in the days when I was teaching at weekend workshops with young would-be actors, when they arrived for the first class I would always say to them, 'Would you like to be an actor? Or do you have to be an actor? Because if you would just like to be an actor, please go and be an accountant. But if you have to be an actor, then at least you'll have the fire that you'll need to overcome some of the problems.' One girl, when I asked her why she wanted to be an actor, said, 'Because I want to get famous, so that I can save seals.' That was the single most bizarre motive that I have ever come across.

I recall a young man who came for a weekend workshop. We talked a little, and it transpired that he had grown up in the country and that he had never ever been to the theatre, or read a play, in his life. I said, 'I don't quite see how you can want to be an actor if at the age of seventeen you've never even been to see a play. I think what you need to do, now you are in London, is to take yourself off to see a play in the West End. You can get yourself a seat in the gods very cheaply.' He wanted to know what I thought he should see, but I told him to look through

the listings in *Time Out* or something, read the descriptions, and decide for himself.

We met again for the next lesson. He was beside himself, with all the shining-eyed ecstasy of the born-again. He said, 'I've been! It is wonderful! I had the best evening! The best time!'

I said, 'Oh, this is great. I'm so delighted. What did you go and see?'

'The Mousetrap!'

But I thought, 'If that's what it takes to turn one person on to the theatre, to go and see more plays, then good old Agatha. That's fine by me.' He was never going to be an actor, this lad, but I hope that he is now a regular theatre-goer and gets great pleasure from it.

From *A Passionate Life* by Stephanie Cole, published by AvonAngliA

Richard Alston

**Plunge, Strange Company,
Lachrymae and Soda Lake**
November, 2001

How did you start out in dance?

At school I had a passion for music, and when I left I went to art college and had a very good visual training, and it was only after those two things that I realised I was actually in love with dance, that it was movement that really inspired me and that I wanted to get my hands dirty with. So I went to the very beginnings of London Contemporary Dance school, even before The Place; it was a very exciting time because it's wonderful when things are just beginning, so it was a classic example of being in the right place at the right time.

My roots and my knowledge are all about contemporary dance, and that's what I deeply love — nothing against ballet, but I don't know nearly as much about it. It's wonderful for me to be back where I used to train, in the studios where I used to get hot and sweaty, working with contemporary trained dancers on my own work. It's been a huge inspiration to me and the most exciting time of my career.

Has that early visual training influenced your choreography?

Yes. I'm really interested in the sculptural, three-dimensional quality of dance. Sometimes the dancers say: 'Do you realise how good it looks when we're in the wings?' — and I know it does; I hope it looks wonderful from the front, too, but it doesn't all just face out; it's all about the wonderful volume of space that the body can push its way into, and the way that dancers can wrap around each other in a duet which gives a marvellous sense of caring and co-operation, and that, I think, is quite sculptural. When I'm dealing with weight, which I often am because I think it makes movement very

deeply centred and therefore very expressive, I think of Henry Moore; Moore is quite an inspiration to me — the way he uses these marvellous shapes and the anatomical nature of his work, the fact that it looks like joints and bones and big curved shapes surrounding each other. He was an artist who was around a lot when I was a child and a young man, and he's had a big influence on me.

Music is important, too, isn't it?

It's always music that inspires me, the connection between movement and music: seeing how close that involvement can become, and then pulling away from it so that it doesn't just become dead and lifeless; playing with the extraordinary effect that music can have on you emotionally as well. That, I would say, is the simplest way to describe the work: that it is full of movement, quite dense — I really like to push dance to the edge, sometimes to almost beyond what people can take in, and then pull it back again. But I also really want people to see and hear — I want to open their ears with what they're seeing and open their eyes with what they're hearing.

How do you find your dancers?

They come to take class with the company or they write to me and sometimes we have auditions. I find auditions very hard because they're such blunt occasions and we're talking about a family; this company is a family, and you don't audition people to be a member of that. It's very important that they're musical; of course they must have a certain amount of physical skill otherwise the dance will be too hard for them, but also I love something individual about each dancer — I don't want them to be all the same height, making a line; I'm looking for people who can make

movement look special in their particular way. I want them to be themselves on stage, not anodyne, anonymous non-beings; that to me is engrossing, and I feel it's engrossing for an audience.

I laugh at myself because I'm often accused of choosing excessively pretty people; it's not what's foremost in my mind, although I do like to look at beautiful people doing amazing things. I am inspired by the idea of human beings challenging and pushing themselves. I don't want people to show off, I don't want people to feel that the dancers are pleased they can do things which are more difficult than other people. I just want the dancing to be clear, and I want it to be fast because it's wonderful to see that sense of flying, of a soul at large, a free spirit.

How do you go about making a piece?

There's some kind of gut response that I have to a piece of music; I know that I would like to make something with it, and then I live with it for months. With the Shostakovich that I'm working on at the moment, I bought seven different recordings so I could get a real sense of how it could be played in different ways before I understood what it was that I liked about the music and chose a particular recording to work with. Then I go into the studio and start making movement, asking for something, working with dancers who know me, who say 'perhaps we could take it this way, what happens if it falls down here and comes up the other side?' And I begin to get a sense of what's working that day, then I can go home and think. I'm building the piece all the time, like building bricks. Not like an architect, making a big drawing beforehand, but having the structure and inspiration of the music, then making my living object piece by piece as it grows. If I realise I've put a piece in the wrong place, that I've made a mistake, then I go back and say I'm sorry, it's not a duet, actually let's pare it down and make it a solo because that's what will make the whole piece work.

What do you like audiences to get from your work?

I think going along to be visually entertained is a blooming healthy place to start. When we go to the theatre to see a play, somebody talks to us and we instantly start thinking about an idea or a narrative in a very literal, specific way, which is what words and thoughts can achieve. There's something more ambiguous, more poetic about dance: it can affect you emotionally, it can affect you very deeply,

but if you're looking for the kind of clarity that's in a play or in a book, it's very confusing. What I hope not to hear too often is people asking what it was about; if people see something in it and they actually relate to it and make something of it for themselves — and it may be something quite different from what I'm thinking — that's fine. It's interesting that there have been pieces I've made quite recently, quite personal pieces, and people in the audience have come up to me and said 'Oh yes — I've been through that.' And I've no idea what they've been through but I'm very happy that they've found something in it. So enjoying dance for the pleasure it gives, for the musical and visual pleasure, that's a terrific way to start; then you might get something different from it.

Who has influenced you?

Fonteyn was a huge influence on me. She was an extraordinary dancer, such a self-effacing performer who showed you the choreography and that was a huge inspiration to me. She had a wonderfully proportioned body; she made physical sense, she made musical sense of everything — she was consummately musical — this is all sounding a bit like a nun but at the same time she had a marvellous contact with the audience, she could play with the audience and of any performer I think I've ever seen, you could not take your eyes off her. I wasn't so inspired by Nuryev because he was more of a look-at-me sort of dancer, so it really was Fonteyn because I think I look for that kind of concentration and integrity in all the dancers I work with. Now we can preserve things on film and video, so there's a whole range of experience that you can begin to understand and watch; dance doesn't just disappear as it once did and that will have an immense effect on the way that it develops.

What do you enjoy when you're not working?

I read a lot, I'm afraid I eat a lot. I hesitate to say that I drink a lot but I do like good wine, and I love company, to be with a group of people and just chat about ordinary things. It's important to get away; you can't be an artist 24 hours a day. I try to go to galleries, I love to go to concerts where music has nothing to do with dance — I go to see *St Matthew's Passion* and I have no desire to choreograph it so that's wonderful. But it is all the arts; they are an amazing affirmation of what humankind can reach for and achieve and it's hard for me to understand people who are uninterested in that. It's impossible for me not to think of culture as a really important part of life.

Belinda Lang

Life x3
by Yasmina Reza
November, 2001

Andrew Blackwood

General Manager, 1958 – 1990

Ex-naval Commander Andrew Blackwood began his lengthy association with Cambridge Arts Theatre in the early months of 1958, taking over responsibility for administration and finance, staffing, public relations and catering from Norman Higgins, the Theatre's long-serving Managing Director and Trustee. Initially, the task of programming remained with Higgins, Andrew Blackwood's only previous experience of theatre having been acquired through his enthusiasm for the amateur world; his passion for the stage in general and the Arts Theatre in particular, however, enabled him to learn the ropes and make the necessary contacts in a short space of time, and he was soon pursuing a successful mixed-programme policy of his own, one which upheld the Theatre's founding loyalties to the five art forms of drama, opera, ballet, music and film, and which provided the city with a calendar of entertainment as appealing as it was eclectic.

Throughout his long tenure as the Arts Theatre's General Manager, Andrew Blackwood proved himself to be a great enabler, nurturing talent and creating a welcoming and supportive atmosphere in which it could experiment and grow: 'At a time when I needed to feel that I belonged, the friendly staff at the Arts unwittingly encouraged me to go on acting after university, so that I could join their family of theatre people,' wrote Sir Ian McKellen in his foreword to a book to mark the Arts' sixtieth anniversary, and in that he voiced a sentiment widely shared by those who were fortunate enough to have gained their first taste of the stage under the watchful eye of Blackwood and George Rylands. Paying homage to the historical precedent set by Maynard Keynes and followed by Higgins and Rylands, Blackwood took the best of University and town talent and mixed it with productions from top-quality producing houses such as Oxford and Nottingham, and touring opera and ballet companies; with tight negotiation, he was also instrumental in bringing pre-London productions to Cambridge, frequently battling with sympathetic but hard-nosed producers to

ensure that contracts were viable and that the Arts was able to compete with larger theatres in attracting shows. The desire to blend established mainstream with home-grown risk, past with future, was cemented during Blackwood's time at the helm in a way which remains unique amongst regional theatres.

Andrew Blackwood's other great dream was to re-establish the sort of Cambridge-based repertory company that the Theatre had experienced with Norman Marshall and the Company of Four: through imagination and determination, he was able to overcome the problems of space and finance which limited the Arts' potential as a producing venue by establishing a series of 'part-time' resident companies: links were first of all made with the Oxford-based Prospect Theatre Company, then came its smaller-scale offshoot, Cambridge Theatre Company (later Method & Madness); established in 1970, CTC became one of the most respected and influential touring companies in the country, enjoying enormous loyalty in its hometown, transfers to the West End and seasons with Zoë Wanamaker, Sheila Hancock, Sian Phillips, Maureen Lipman and Ian Charleson.

Whilst juggling many duties, Blackwood never forgot the importance of safeguarding the Theatre's future: he formed Cambridge Arts Theatre's Youth Group to develop new audiences and, throughout the serious financial difficulties that dogged the Arts Theatre from the 1960s to the 1980s, Blackwood fought long and hard for its survival, simultaneously inspiring in others a great belief that the battle was worthwhile. With Rylands, he established an endowment Fund in memory of Keynes, and the two led a larger-scale appeal in 1982 which raised £600,000; the presence of stars such as Peggy Ashcroft, Judi Dench,

Andrew Blackwood pictured with his successor Stephen Walton.

Trevor Nunn, Ian McKellen, Prunella Scales and Timothy West at the Theatre's 50th anniversary fundraising gala testified to the enormous respect and affection in which the Arts was held.

Widely known and celebrated for what director Richard Cottrell called his 'admirable eccentricities', Andrew Blackwood was a colourful man presiding over a colourful time, a period in the Theatre's history in which fire and flood, bloody battles with knives between chefs and the theft of the Trust's entire stock of Chateau d'Yquem were as much in a day's work as box office figures and audience development. Ever courteous, he approached it all with a practical good-humour, never once forgetting that 'The play is really the thing, and nothing beats the thrill of curtain-up on opening night.' He saw upwards of a thousand of those, continuing to support the Arts Theatre long after his retirement and, despite his inherent modesty, many of today's performers and directors would attribute their success at least in part to his gentle encouragement. His is a quiet but lasting legacy, appreciated by all who continue to enjoy live performance at the theatre to which he was devoted.

Pete Postlethwaite

Scaramouche Jones
by Justin Butcher
June, 2002

What interests you most about the part of Scaramouche Jones?

It wasn't so much the part, initially, as the scale of the piece. Scaramouche Jones is a metaphor as much as a person in his own right, a cipher for the whole of the twentieth century and a kind of Candide figure, an Everyman who goes from 1899 to 1999 with an extraordinary acceptance of what happens to him. I felt that both in the character and in the piece there was a plea for compassion, a desire just to take a rain-check on how we treat each other.

The play takes place in a dimly-lit backstage area of some kind of fairground, with ropes and tables and a tumbler and a mirror; there's a crucifixion and other odd things scattered about, and it's obviously the corner of a circus that the hundred year-old clown has used for the last fifty years to change and put his make-up on. When the show starts, you see him coming off stage for the last time and facing up to the ghosts around him, spectres and images that have haunted him for the last hundred years, in an effort to find out what will be the consequence of his life; it's like Peer Gynt's onion – if he strips away all the layers, what will be underneath? Will there be a soul? Will there be something worthwhile?

Justin Butcher clearly loves biography and you love stories; it must have been a match made in heaven?

It felt very much like that. He's a deeply humanitarian person, with an extraordinary care for people and why people matter. At the same time, he has a fascination for pictorial and historical detail. Some of this story is personal to him: his mother was Trinidadian, which is where Scaramouche is born; his uncles were Poles who knew the present pope; the judge that Scaramouche is eventually reprieved by from the concentration camp

was actually his great-grandfather at the trials of Nuremberg; so there's a personal history woven in. He was also thinking about what Englishness meant in the twentieth century. What have we done? We've had the holocaust and within two years of the Millennium we had September 11th and you think – what has changed? Nothing – we're on the same road.

You were Oscar-nominated for your role as Giuseppe Conlon in *In the Name of the Father*; the part was something you wanted very badly – why?

Because I agreed with it. I identified with the injustice that was being examined, and I recognised in the character a quintessential part of my own father, who was exactly the same, and who would have behaved in exactly the same way as Conlon, even though he was northern English as opposed to northern Irish – a very firm, strong-believing Catholic. He died in 1988, so there was some kind of atonement going on; some kind of feeling of I can see you dad, I know what you're doing.

Many will remember you as Danny, in *Brassed Off*; the film was a wonderful slice of English history – did you enjoy it?

Incredibly, and again there's a synchronicity between what I feel – personally, spiritually and politically – and what Mark Herman was trying to say in *Brassed Off* or what Jim Sheridan was trying to say with *In the Name of the Father*. I don't deny I'm a political animal, although I'm not a member of any political party. There are things I feel very strongly about and that I've followed, and the twin injustices of the Guildford Four and the Birmingham Six and what happened to the miners in the hand-bagging years of Thatcher was extraordinary. When you get the opportunity to use whatever ability you have as an actor to fulfil somebody's vision, it's wonderful – it's form and content coming together and creating a beautiful whole.

Maddy Prior

November, 2001

You've had an amazingly varied musical career spanning more than 35 years, but you started out as a chauffeur, didn't you?

Well, I did. I drove the Revd. Gary Davies around for a month which was a baptism by fire. He was wonderful and very interesting, but what a culture shock! I'd never dealt with anybody blind, black or a blues singer, or old! He was classic and great fun, but it was extraordinary to travel England in the mid 1960s with someone like him. Then I drove some Americans around who finally convinced me that I ought to sing English music, not American. I joined up with Tim [Hart] soon after that and it went into Steeleye and then diverged into other things.

Your work with Tim was interesting because it was perhaps the first time that anybody had bothered to look for character songs as opposed to 'Blowin' in the Wind' and all the protest stuff that was going round.

Those songs are interesting to listen to now because they're so naïve in some ways but they pulled into an area of traditional music that was starting to enjoy a revival, particularly with Martin Carthy. I started to realise then that history was interesting – I'd always hated it at school – and Eleanor of Aquitaine became one of my favourite characters, so songs like that came to life for me.

After you and Tim had toured and introduced people to those songs, Steeleye Span blew the folk industry apart, but the formation of the band didn't go smoothly, did it?

No, but then what does?! Tim and I were like an also-ran choice, about tenth on the list if choice had been involved but it isn't often and we happened to be in the same house; it was juxtaposition that landed us in that situation. It was based around Ashley Hutchings and Terry and Gay Woods – they needed more people and we wanted to give it a whirl because we were definitely interested in electric; the problem was finance, and Ashley had access to that so we were lucky; that house in Whitehall Park was a stopping place for lots of musicians, a good place to be. We foolishly got it together in the country for three months which is something I'd never advise any band to do because there's nothing like being isolated with people you don't know to find any friction there may be – and we did find it. We managed to make the album, which was something of an achievement, but split immediately after that and it was generally felt that the thing was finished. But it was a shame and Tim revived it by asking Martin if he was interested in the project and he said yes; he brought to it his inimitable style and really worked on that area of riffs, largely based on pipes, that he uses on the guitar, and that gave it the kick up the bum that it needed. Later we brought in drums which was another kind of direction and difference, and in lots of ways harder to deal with because drums are very difficult with traditional music: the music will not be denied and neither will the drums.

It didn't take long for Steeleye Span to become stars of their own race as the folk rock movement became widely accepted and people discovered that you could take the most amazing folk ballads and instead of singing them to fifty people in a folk club, perform to five or six thousand people in the Rainbow Theatre. The one thing that Steeleye did, though, which other bands didn't, was to produce stage shows – not just music – that were genuinely different.

I love the whole ethos of performing. The music is one aspect of it but I'm not a purist in any way so I also loved using other elements like dance, theatre and costume – we used the ribbons from the mummers plays – and bringing them in to what we did. The folk world was very anti-theatre; I didn't know if this was because Ewan [MacColl] had been involved in theatre, but it sees dramatic elements as tricks; I see them as colour that lends a vitality to the work, which can help make it accessible to people who might not know anything about the music.

And the moment in a Steeleye show that people always looked forward to was when you ran into the audience…

Yes, although I think I used to run off adrenaline! I used to be so nervous that I'd run to the top of the theatres when they had several balconies, and I think it's the only thing that's kept me fit over the years. It was a release for me from being up on stage. One of my favourite times was in Santa Monica Civic Theatre, when the bouncers obviously hadn't seen me come off because they wouldn't let me back on again.

As a woman and the focal point of a band, you had to make choices between life in and out of the music; you married Rick Kemp, the bass player in the band, and children were next on the agenda – but at a time when you were at the height of your success.

The old biological clock does tick on and so I became pregnant and the whole of the eighties, for me, although I was involved with three different bands, were largely channelled towards juggling Alex and touring; Alex came with me on the road most of the time, but when we moved north and had Rose, they tended to stay at home and Rick left the band to be there more, too. So it has been a juggling

act but if you're a working mum, whatever your job, there's no way round it and even being able to afford nannies doesn't change things a great deal – it makes it practically possible, but you still have all the emotions and guilt.

The Carnival Band was a curious choice of collaborator.

I was asked to put a vocal on five tracks they'd put down – I think they'd looked at what my range was but I don't know what they'd listened to because they were incredibly high and fast! Anyway, it happened again the following year and the year after that so somebody said we should do an album, which we did in a wonderful Quaker Meeting House down in Bristol; that was rather fun so we went out on tour and it sort of rolled on in a gentle way from there. Then we wanted to do something besides sacred songs so we did seventeenth-century drinking songs just to make the point! They're wonderful to work with because they're terribly witty, both musically and verbally, and their point of view is wonderfully fresh and free, they're not hidebound by anything that they know – and that I find truly delightful.

One of your much-loved collaborations was with June Tabor as Silly Sisters – how did that come about?

June and I had known each other for years and we both lived in North London. We started by singing Bulgarian music together initially, which has stamped the whole way we've approached music together – anything that went jangly was always a good idea for us! We did a few clubs and then made a lovely album, and it was really the first time that folk musicians had been let loose in a studio with a fully-fledged engineer and all the outboard and stuff that was available then – otherwise it had been on less versatile equipment, well done but not as sophisticated. We could have more people on, more separation of sounds, better reverbs – stuff that makes it sound better without people knowing why. And some of the best people around to work with, so that was lovely to do. Thirteen years later, June moved in around the corner and we did a second album, very different in style and approach to the first. Tracks from that like 'Agincourt' and 'Love and Gold' are lovely pieces to play, really smashing.

Looking back now on your career so far, what are some personal highlights for you?

Well, there is one which is nothing to do with the performing. I was in Australia not long ago and Johnny Rotten was in the bar, so I rang home and they wanted me to get his autograph; I didn't want to because we'd all been avoiding him like the plague but I thought I'd better, so I got it and went back to my room. Then I thought, there must be a conversation there so I went back down and there was just him and his pals sitting there talking. I tried to join in and they looked with irritation at this middle-aged woman being a nuisance, but I wasn't going to be intimidated so I stayed and eventually he asked me what band I was in; I told him

it was Steeleye Span, and he went 'oh my word, now I'm really embarrassed'. I was just gob-smacked because that was such kudos for the band, and it was just one of those extraordinary moments.

What's it like having Rick and now Rose with you on stage?

It's great to be with Rick because he's such a wonderful bass player and we haven't had the chance to work together much in these last few years. Rose is extraordinary: she's still a teenager but older than I am – very mature and a lovely singer, very musical; she's delightful to work with – most of the time!

Maddy Prior and Rose Kemp

Neil Pearson

The Real Thing
by Tom Stoppard
November, 2001

Christopher Biggins

Over the course of five years, Christopher Biggins directed and starred in the most successful Christmas shows that the Arts Theatre has ever enjoyed: *Mother Goose* (1999-2000); *Jack and the Beanstalk* (2000-1); *Dick Whittington and His Cat* (2001-2); *Cinderella* (2002-3); and *Aladdin* (2003-4).

You've had an extraordinary career which has bounced around every genre in the industry; where did the young Christopher Biggins come from?

I was born in Oldham, which I'm very proud of even though I only spent three weeks there. I came down to Salisbury in the back of a Pickford's lorry, wrapped in cotton wool, which I still have an aversion to.

What about schooling?

One of the regrets I have is that I never went to university. From school, I went straight to rep, which was fantastic, and then to drama school. But school started me off in the theatrical way because my Great Auntie Vi insisted that I talk posh Queen's English instead of this wonderful Wiltshire burr, so I had elocution lessons. Mrs Christian at school was marvellous and she got me interested in theatre and saw something there; so did my music teacher, Mr Lewis. I was doing plays at thirteen — *The Pirates of Penzance* and even an Ethel Merman musical, *Call Me Madam,* in which I played the Ethel Merman part — bizarre, but it gave me a wonderful idea that I'd like to do theatre. Salisbury was blessed with the most fantastic rep company, so at sixteen I went there for two wonderful years, finishing up with an Equity card. Then I went to Bristol Old Vic Theatre School, which was another wonderful experience because suddenly I was mixing with my own age group — daunting but also exhilarating.

Lots of people think of you as a children's entertainer, but there's a serious side to your work, for example you had a spell at the RSC with Judi Dench.

I did — it was fantastic. I did a play called *Love and Assurance* with Judi, Elizabeth Spriggs and Donald Sinden — it was a big hit, and I did other plays for them afterwards. Because I became a personality, people forget I've played Nero in *I Claudius* and the sex-crazed vicar Ossie Whitworth in *Poldark* — both of which were great TV shows. *I Claudius* still stands as a masterful work, just superb.

What was it like to work on?

Believe it or not, Nero only comes into the last episode and it was a very small cast by then because everyone was dead! But there was a fantasy sequence when Derek Jacobi was hallucinating and all the major stars — John Hurt, Sian Phillips — came back to do a dream sequence. It was very special to be involved in a series like that.

What are your memories of *Poldark*?

There are lots of great memories and Winston Graham, who wrote the novels, became a great friend. The whole thing took nine months and we were down in Cornwall for three, which was just idyllic. It was nice to do good drama with good scripts — I wish they'd do more on television now.

In *Porridge,* you played Lukewarm with another outstanding cast.

Ronnie Barker is the king of all situation comedies. He's a real comedy *actor*, and very generous. We didn't change much of the scripts because they were superb, but occasionally Ronnie would say 'you take my line because it's funnier that way' — his generosity was enormous. At the end of the first series he gave all the regulars a silver tankard with 'Slade Prison 1974' and our characters' names on it; he gave me an initial so it reads 'Lukewarm P.' — which sums up his sense of humour.

What's the secret of its success?

Good writing, good direction, good acting — it was original and it was funny. Some of the things that are on now shouldn't be called comedies because there are no laughs. The public should have more choice about what they watch — sometimes they're subjected to things that aren't good for the sake of money; television now is completely run by accountants. When I first did *Surprise, Surprise,* we got audiences of fifteen million; now the only shows that get that are things like *Coronation Street.*

Which is one programme you haven't touched yet…

No, but I have some very good friends in it and it's the only programme I religiously record every week.

You've influenced a whole generation of viewers through children's television — how important is that?

Very, and it's the same with panto. I'm quite strict because it's no good just throwing a pantomime on — you have to tell a story, you have to tell it well, you have to include the audience, because many have never been to a live show before. You've got to make it really special because you want them to come back the next year, and wouldn't it be nice if they came to the theatre in between? Not to be terribly grand about it, but it's a very important learning process for everybody — children and adults. There's still a taboo that theatre is for a certain type of person, but you can be intellectual, lowest of the low, middle class and still enjoy panto.

As well as starring in the show, you also direct each pantomime — how much planning does that involve?

Well, we start thinking about each panto when we're doing the one before, and all through the year something is going on, whether it be casting, travelling to see the sets, getting the wardrobe people involved or working on the script — so it's a twelve-month business. It's been wonderful to achieve such success here. Panto is a real tradition in cities like Cambridge, and audiences like to come back and see regular people; because they like what they've seen, they book almost immediately for the next year. We have gags that we keep in every year and part of the fun is that people will join in with them almost before I've opened my mouth — and that is exciting, to have such a following.

What do you enjoy when you're not working?

I love visiting different countries and I'm lucky because my partner works for British Airways, so we travel an awful lot. I adore cooking and entertaining and being entertained; I love art, and over the years I've collected quite a good group of paintings. I like television, reading, going to the cinema and I'm an avid theatre-goer.

Your personal circle of friends includes Joan Collins and Cilla Black; what is it about you that makes you so accessible to people who have to be careful who their friends are?

Well, I like people for a start — there's nothing better for me than to be able to spend time with friends. I get criticised by the press for going to the opening of a letter, and I like to go out but I'm not forced into it, I don't ring people and say where's the party? Friends are very important — they're the best in life, and I'm blessed with a very wide range. Joan is amazing — I've never known a woman with energy like her; she's incredibly funny and we're absolute ace scrabble players.

Who wins?

We both do. We're both quite tough and we know how each other plays. Whenever we have a moment, we sit down and play and we do love it. But I have lots of friends in all sorts of fields, and that's the other thing — I never think of who people are or if they can help me, I just love people.

Leslie Phillips

Naked Justice
by John Mortimer
March, 2002

Your role in *Naked Justice* includes a little bit of all the things we know you for: there's the cad and the bounder, but there's also a lot of depth.

Well, John writes so beautifully deeply but in a light way; he's got comedy coming out of his pores, and the most amazingly sharp mind. This part is a lot of him, a lot of the humanity that he finds in his work

You're from a Cockney family, which is perhaps not what people would expect from somebody as well-spoken as yourself, and the first role you ever played was a wolf?

Yes. I've gone up the most extraordinary roads in life and a lot of them have been following my nose — very few I've made up my mind to do. The first time I earned money as an actor was as a wolf in *Peter Pan*, then I was in films as a kid in the 1930s; life moved on and the war came, but I was in theatre right up until I went into the army in 1942 — I was in a play with Vivien Leigh at that time. I was invalided out of the army about three years later, then crept back to the theatre and started wandering around all the old haunts in Shaftesbury Avenue. Theatre was what it was all about for me, and I did have this extraordinary grounding that nobody gets anymore and that nobody will ever get again; I learned my job thoroughly, and the people who taught me were great people.

You had a terrible war, didn't you?

Well, it wasn't too bad. What was good about it was that I didn't do any entertaining. I got stuck into becoming an officer, really because I looked like one — I sort of suited the part, and so I got my commission in the Royal Artillery and

was immediately transferred to the Infantry. I had quite a difficult time, in a way, but I didn't want to piddle around doing shows for the troops; I was in the army, so I was going to be in the army. When I came out, there was plenty of work to be had because it was just before the end of the war and so I beat the field, just as I beat the field going in — I got wonderful jobs when I was seventeen and eighteen because there weren't any people around with trousers.

The British comedy network threw up the most amazing collection of English actors at that time, and actors of a very special sort; we were very lucky.

The thing then was that comedy had a special place, but it wasn't a very high place — drama was always considered acting and comedy was messing about, so people thought you were either a funny person or a serious person. Of course, there was no television then which is how comedy got its advancement; when people realised how important it was to have people in these funny little boxes who could make others laugh and enjoy their lives, it became a great art.

You've played many different sorts of roles, particularly recently — has that been somebody trying to get out?

I think it was more somebody trying to get back, because I did so many sorts of parts as I grew up and it never struck me for a moment that I was going to be a funny man; I was really rather a serious boy, and it was only later that I realised I was getting drawn into a comedy kind of career. Once you can play comedy, once you have a sense of timing and can say hello in a way that makes people fall on their face, they want you to do it again and again and again. Then you realise you're developing some kind of thing that isn't

you at all; it's as much a character part as playing Falstaff. I can turn that on and turn it off now, it doesn't really matter, but most people want me to say some of those comedy things.

Do you get fed up with that?

It depends where they do it! I travel a lot by tube and I get recognised and people inevitably ask me to say those phrases, but I don't mind too much. I think what I've managed is to do things that are about life, which is full of both comedy and drama; they're the roles I've enjoyed most.

Radio days were very important to you, too — and you certainly had the voice for it.

I've always done radio. That's all there was: you were in the theatre, you made a film occasionally and you did radio. Television, strangely enough, has been less of my life than for most people. I made my name through radio and film and theatre — but I'm a theatre actor, really. You used to say I'm going on the stage; now people say I'm going to be an actor because most don't go on the stage; it's so important to do so, though, because you contact the audience and you can use that contact when you're making a film or doing television where there is no audience. All actors should learn about the theatre; sadly, not all of them do. When you hear every word that someone says, you know they're a theatre actor. As for the voice, I'm lucky, because I've got good diction and your job is to make sure the audience gets every word from the author — that's what I try to do.

Are there any people in particular that you'll always remember working with?

So many, because from the ages of ten to eighteen I worked with people like Seymour Hicks, Vivien Leigh, Rex Harrison, John Gielgud and Marie Tempest, and top singers, too, because I went to Covent Garden for a couple of operas. They were so kind and so helpful — they loved to show us things and tell us what to do and what not to do, although we didn't always listen. As a child and a teenager, people were terribly good to us; actors took time, and it was through them that I learned to speak properly. I developed an accent by virtue of the people I worked with.

What about leading ladies?

There's one glaring lady who was so wonderful, who got me a job in Hollywood, and that was Kay Kendall; she was the most wonderful, delightful woman and I find it very hard to get over the fact that, during the time I was working with her, she was dying; in fact, she died a couple of years after making that movie. She was quite special; she opened doors for me everywhere, and I was allowed to take her about by her husband, Rex Harrison, who I'd also worked with; he would say 'You can go out with Leslie — he's all right'; little did he know I'd grown up!

Where's home for you?

London. I'm a Londoner born and bred, and I've never wanted to live anywhere else. I like to go all over the place and I love my place in Spain, but it's only for short bursts; it inspires me to write and grow, and I get time to think there, but I don't have those retirement thoughts of staying there.

What would a perfect day off consist of?

I'd get up late. I hate getting up early, although I'm very good at it and very determined; when I made all those films I was up at five and made up at eight, and I do like to work hard and get cracking and get it done. But if I had nothing to do all day, I'd probably answer some fan letters — I never quite get on top of those, although I always reply in the end. I'm never idle.

Wendy Craig

The Circle
by W. Somerset Maugham
October, 2002

You've just come off stage in Somerset Maugham's *The Circle:* it's the sort of play that everyone can enjoy, and your role, Lady Kitty, is a wonderful creation.

Yes, she's a wonderfully attractive social butterfly, both funny and touching, who's lived for the moment and run off with her lover, then come back to England. Life hasn't been what she thought it was going to be, and she's a little saddened and embittered by the whole experience, but what I really love about her is that she still maintains her *joie de vivre*. The play is about her coming back home to find that her son's wife is about to do just the same thing. There are so many twists and turns, and it's the most beautifully constructed play because you never really know until the very end what is going to happen. It's a period piece, and everything that's discussed is about the law in those days, but it's really a play about relationships, a romance which takes a cynical look at life, at what people get up to and the games they play. And the same things happen today — it still speaks to us.

Do you enjoy period drama, because looking at your most recent work there's been *The Forsyte Saga, The Rivals* and now *The Circle*?

Actually, I just like to work, so if I'm offered something like that then I'm happy to do it, but there's something very attractive about seeing the clothes that people wore and looking at the way they lived their lives, and I loved being in *The Forsyte Saga.* We did shoot a whole lot more but, because there were only six episodes, there wasn't time to show it all so those who weren't involved in the main storyline got the chop.

You were Britain's favourite mother many years ago, always in a family drama on TV. *Butterflies* in particular was quite special, a milestone in British television — we still enjoy it now, and it continues to strike a note with married women.

I loved playing Ria. It was beautifully written and cast. It rang a lot of bells for people, and they could identify with all the characters, really — the married couple, the sons were very real and the youngsters associated themselves with them, and the story can be told over and over again for many years to come: it's a timeless story of people becoming unsettled in marriage. It's almost like *The Circle* — but Ria didn't run off, whereas Lady Kitty did.

It moved beautifully from extreme comedy to poignant drama, and that doesn't happen so much these days.

Yes, they dared to show more depth in those days; they dared to be serious, and that's the best sort of comedy, where you're not quite sure whether you're laughing or crying — the very finest.

You followed *Butterflies* with *Nanny*, something very different; you were personally involved in the development of that series, weren't you?

Yes, it was my idea. I was catching a train home to see my mother and I stopped to pick up a magazine and I was in a hurry so I just grabbed one; it turned out to be *The Lady*, and it had a lot of adverts in the back pages — people wanting to be nannies, people looking for nannies — and I read down this list and thought what an interesting thing it must be and that it would perhaps make a good play. When I did some research into it with my husband, we found that there was enough material to sustain a series, so I wrote

down a format and character and story-line ideas and sent it in under the pseudonym 'Jonathan Marr', because I didn't think anybody would take it seriously if they knew it was scatty Wendy Craig! But my agent rang three months later and said the BBC wanted to do it — I was overwhelmed with joy to be in at the beginning of something like that, and to be on the creative side as well as performing.

It was filmed in and around Southwold; that's such a beautiful location — and one that you were already familiar with.

I do love that beautiful little seaside resort, and of course I was in rep at Ipswich. Those years were tremendously important and I do think repertory theatre is the best possible training ground for an actor: if you get through your time in rep and survive it and learn from it, you're going to be all right for the rest of your career because it's very tough; you're playing at night, rehearsing something else during the day, learning lines on the run, and maybe you're an assistant stage manager as well. You really learn the business, and it can't be done in any other way. It worries me that there are very few reps now and I just don't know where the young actors are training. Getting as much experience playing different parts in different plays is what really matters.

You started your career by appearing in films that are now becoming the signposts of British film-making — *The Servant*, for example, for which you got an award and played alongside Dirk Bogarde and James Fox; what are your memories of that time?

Film was terribly important in those days and taken very seriously. *The Servant* was directed by Joseph Losey, who was one of the best American directors, and he was very serious, believe me! There were no laughs and everything had to be perfect: you couldn't even chew a sweet between shots without him looking a little put out. But it was very exciting: you knew that what you were doing was being photographed by the best cinematographer, that there would be the best art director — and the script was wonderfully written by Harold Pinter. Everything was done to perfection.

How did you find your leading men?

Well, Dirk was delightful and James was very young and inexperienced, but a charming man. Dirk was so kind to me; he was extremely experienced and a top actor, and yet he had time to show me the ropes because I didn't know anything about filming technique and he explained it all to me very patiently — the roles and how different shots were done. He was very kind.

Were you ever tempted to throw your lot in with Hollywood, because that was an extraordinary piece of acting?

No, not really. I was married, and lived in England with a child and I didn't really want to go to America at all. But it wasn't just that, of course — I wasn't asked, because I wasn't the sort of girl they had in films in America in those days. I've never been a beauty and they liked conventional beauty on the screen back then so it was never an option. English actresses are much more down to earth — they settle for what they are.

How would you spend a complete day off?

How would I get one?! But if I did, I'd pray for a sunny day and spend it in my garden, looking at the flowers and walking in the fields behind my house.

I know that you've published one or two cookery books in your time, so presumably — unlike Ria — you can cook?

Yes, I can actually. My mother taught me to cook when I was very young — I could cook the Sunday roast for the family by the time I was thirteen. I'm a plain cook, not a *cordon bleu* chef, but I can turn out a decent meal, believe it or not!

You've spent years entertaining us — what entertains you?

Oh, music, definitely — classical music. I just love it, and I have it all the time. Whenever I want to relax or find peace from all the noise and bustle that goes on, I put on music.

Sian Phillips

The Old Ladies
by Rodney Ackland
October, 2003

Your public life began as a broadcaster; what sort of thing did you broadcast?

Children's hour, mostly, or poetry readings and features. Then I graduated to doing grown-up plays like *Saturday Night Theatre*, which was a big thrill to do. When I was seventeen, I worked as an announcer as well, and I used to travel with the BBC Concert Orchestra, writing their scripts and introducing them.

You moved on to university to study English and philosophy; English is important for any actress, but why did you choose philosophy?

When I got to university I had to have a fill-in subject and everyone was doing education. The queue was so long to sign up that I decided against it; there was no queue for philosophy, so I joined and fell madly in love with it. It was supposed to be just for a year, but I ended up doing three years and taking my degree in it because I loved it so much. The only useful things I've ever learned are Latin, philosophy and physical training – the rest has been no use at all!

A lot of people will remember you in *I Claudius* – do you have good memories of that series?

I've only seen it once myself. It always seems to be on in America, but very rarely in Britain. It was an interesting piece of work, but it seemed to go on for months with lots of rehearsals and shoots at the weekend. We had all worked together before, so we knew each other and it was fun, but we never thought it would be as popular as it turned out to be.

You've toured extensively in a show about Marlene Dietrich; were you a fan?

Not of her movies, but I did see the cabaret and loved it; it was in Wimbledon in 1975 and I thought she was brilliant.

She was a much cleverer actress in cabaret than she was in films – I think some of the movies are dreadful. I wasn't even a great fan of her look – that perfect, enamelled Hollywood look with not a hair out of place; it was only when I began the show that I found out how much work goes into looking that perfect! She was a genius at make-up and lighting, so I came out of it with an enormous respect for her because she completely re-invented herself in her middle years, which is almost impossible to do, and became even more successful as she got older.

You can't be Marlene without the voice: did your Welsh origins help with that?

I didn't start to sing until 1980 in my first musical, *Pal Joey*; before that, I'd never sung alone. I had my own choir at school in Wales and my father was a singer, so I was brought up in a very musical household, but mostly classical music. I didn't learn about show tunes until I was in them.

Is there one particular role that you're pleased to have worked on?

I've especially enjoyed the Tennessee Williams plays; *The Night of the Iguana* was the one I liked most of all, I just adored playing Hannah. I got to know Tennessee and I just loved acting in his plays.

You move from cabaret to play with the odd radio serial thrown in, not to mention writing a multi-part autobiography; is there such a thing as a day off for you?

I honestly don't remember when I last had a day off. I like going to the pictures, seeing friends and going to restaurants, but it's been so long since I went out to dinner that I can barely remember how to eat with a knife and fork! I love gardening and walking, and I sight-see a lot between shows: I like to potter in and out of buildings.

Glynis Barber

The Graduate

*Original production adapted
and directed by Terry Johnson*

August — September, 2003

You're coming to the part of Mrs. Robinson shortly after playing Lady Macbeth, two very formidable ladies; will you carry any of one over into the other, do you think?

It is interesting to play two parts that are from such different times and cultures yet are both formidable women, but formidable in very different ways: I always think of *Macbeth* as a love story between two people who are very ambitious and make bad choices and therefore destroy that love and the good things they have in their life; Mrs. Robinson is someone who doesn't have any love — hers is the opposite of a love story. It seems to me that she's a very interesting woman — very disappointed, very bitter and very sad, and she comes across quite ferociously but there's such a vulnerability to her. It's an intriguing, fantastic part, because she's so fun to watch and so sexy, but at the same time so interesting: where she is in her life is not a particularly happy place and she has a very strange relationship with her daughter, so there's lots there to explore.

With the array of actresses that have played her on stage recently, were you tempted to go along and see one of those shows?

The Graduate had finished in the West End by the time I was offered this, and I'm quite grateful that I didn't get to see it now because it's quite a daunting array — Kathleen Turner, Anne Archer, Linda Gray, Jerry Hall — and that might have thrown me a bit. I saw the film, but even that was many years ago so it's faded from memory, and I think it's rather nice to take a fresh approach to it. It's the same as playing Lady Macbeth when you know that so many great people have played her; what I tried to do there was wipe my mind clean and really look at the text afresh to bring my own ideas and perceptions to it, which is exactly what I'll do in this. There are many different ways to play Mrs. Robinson, so

I don't know if I'll end up being very different or quite similar to some of the others, but hopefully I'll put my own stamp on it.

A lot has been made of the nudity in the West End — how do you feel about that?

Well, our producer, Sacha Brooks, is very keen that everybody who takes this part is comfortable and does what they want. It's always what the press will jump onto, even though it's a fifteen-second part of what is in fact a fantastic play. We haven't started rehearsals, and there's a very exciting young female director on this which will put a very interesting perspective on it, so to be honest we haven't discussed it; we'll approach that moment when we reach it in rehearsal, and at the moment I don't know how it will turn out.

The music is going to be very evident in the production, and the Simon and Garfunkel soundtrack was very much the soundtrack to the whole era of the film — do you relate to those times?

I remember singing the songs at school very vividly, and I'm sure that for anyone who was around then it will create a very nostalgic feel. Anything set in the 1960s is great because it was such a wonderful decade, but I think the issues in the play are very relevant and modern; a graduate who's done really well has lots of expectations placed upon him and he's meant to fit like a peg into certain holes and live his life in a particular way, even though he may just not feel like that inside. And to be very inexperienced with women and then meet this remarkable, daunting woman, not to know whether to stay or run away — I'm sure every man must go through that at some stage in his life. The issues are completely relevant and I don't think anyone will have problems relating to them.

Sir Donald Sinden

The Hollow Crown

Devised and directed by John Barton

October, 2003

What is *The Hollow Crown* about?

Well, in 1961 in Stratford upon Avon, Peter Hall was running the company and a production was not ready to open, and it wouldn't be ready for another two weeks; they couldn't have the theatre empty, so to keep the curtain up, John Barton — who is a great scholar — went back to his office that afternoon and put together the whole of *The Hollow Crown* from his own head, starting with the Anglo Saxon Chronicles. It's the history of the kings and queens of England in their own words or the words of their contemporaries. It's a wonderful compilation, and it's been done on and off ever since; I've done it with six different leading ladies, including Peggy Ashcroft and Dorothy Tutin, and all of them bring something different to the part.

Did you train professionally?

Yes and no. I started during the war, and it was quite by accident. I joined a company entertaining the forces — it was a wartime job; we all had to do something and I was turned down for the forces because of asthma. I enjoyed it, but I was very much aware that my technique needed polishing, so I went to a voice teacher in Brighton with the resounding name of Leslie Charteris-Coffin, and he maintained that I

was a bass so he pushed my voice down and down and down, and so deep was it that in 1952 they said it was far too deep for the young men that I was playing, so I went to another voice teacher who lightened it by an octave. At the end of the war, I went to a drama school for a year; I knew what I needed to learn, and I'd never done any dancing or fencing so I concentrated on that sort of thing. Then I went out into the big wide world and to Stratford in 1946.

What was Stratford like then?

Wonderful, absolutely wonderful. It was a very exciting company. A man called Sir Barry Jackson had just taken over running the theatre; it was a new broom and he wouldn't have anybody who'd worked at Stratford before, so there were a lot of new young juveniles — John Harrison, who went on to run Birmingham Rep; Paul Schofield — we were all young kids together and it was great fun. We did eight plays in a season, with a month's rehearsal for each play, so once they were all on a member of the audience could arrive at Stratford and see eight different plays in a week. We used to spend the days playing cricket or rowing on the river, then come into the theatre at night and depend on the wardrobe staff; you went into the dressing room and saw the costume for *Henry V* — so on you went for that; you never bothered beforehand to think about it.

You flag up *The Cruel Sea* **as being the favourite film that you've done.**

Yes, I was extremely lucky to have that as my first film and go in at the deep end. When I first started as an actor, the theatre was divided between classical and modern performers; if you were a classical actor, you only worked at Stratford, the Old Vic, Regent's Park; if you were modern, you were in the plays of Noël Coward and Terence Rattigan. Very few people did the crossover; I started as a modern actor, then pulled all the strings I could to get to Stratford, and suddenly I was a classical actor and couldn't get a job in a modern play. Then, in 1952, I became a film actor and discovered there was a third category because I then couldn't get a job in the theatre, so did nothing but films for eight years. Television had started, and there had been the revolution in theatre with the Royal Court and *Look Back in Anger* — so I had to fight to get back in again, and since that moment I've tried to keep a foot in every possible camp.

Working for the Rank Organisation — that was our version of Hollywood, so what was it like?

They were making sixteen feature films a year at Pinewood Studios alone, and they had a stable of which I was one for eight years. They thought towards the end of that time that bringing in some Hollywood stars might pep up the box office a bit, and while I was there Marilyn Monroe came over to do *The Prince and the Showgirl* with Olivier. I had my own dressing room there because I was an old hand, and one day they started knocking two dressing rooms into one because she wanted a bigger room; they decorated the whole thing blue — furniture, carpets, walls — then two weeks before she was due to arrive, a henchman turned up and said 'Marilyn doesn't like blue', so they redecorated it all in white. She arrived, and she never walked anywhere without an entourage — six or seven people always around her. But she was known for being a devotee of the Method School of Acting so one day, for the fun of it, I put a notice on my dressing room door saying that it was the Pinewood branch, stone-kicking a speciality, hands in pockets taught, that sort of silly thing; I suddenly heard the entourage coming down the corridor, and they stopped outside my door — then there was a peel of girlish laughter, my door was thrown open and in she came, slamming the door

behind her, and we talked for forty minutes. She was rather a silly girl, but desperately attractive; it's the saddest thing that she died like that, but those whom the gods love…

TV has been big for you — are there any shows that you're particularly pleased to have been involved with?

Well, I've always maintained that whatever I'm doing next is the best — or whatever I'm doing now; it's the only way to look at it — I don't like looking back. I've made mistakes — we all have — but there's no point in crying over them. TV has the worst elements of film and theatre, you're quite right, but when I started in 1948 it was live TV and terrifying. It's shortened my life by several years, that.

You have a great passion for the theatre and the history side is important to you to; you're connected with the Theatre Museum in Covent Garden, aren't you?

Yes, I was on the committee that started that. Almost anything you could think of had a museum attached to it: there's a museum of fans in London, the Wellcome Institute has a museum for lavatories, so why — with all the artefacts and old stage machinery — isn't there one for theatre? We worked for a long time on that and it eventually opened in 1972, and it's now run under the umbrella of the V & A; it's the most exciting place to go because you can go and see things belonging to people you've heard of and revered. They're doing the most wonderful thing of televising theatrical performances, because otherwise theatre is such an ephemeral business; if only we had a recording of Gielgud's *Hamlet* or Irving's *The Bells*.

What great performances have inspired you?

Donald Wolfit inspired me enormously because I never thought anything could be that big, not just in vocal sound but in sheer size of performance; if you've been to Rome, to the Sistine Chapel and looked at the Doom painting, the *Day of Judgement* at the far end — it's enormous; so if you can imagine seeing that for the first time to the sound of Beethoven's *Ninth Symphony*, watching Wolfit was a bit like that — it was tremendous. Then I came enormously under the influence of an American actor called Alfred Lunt, the finest light comedian I've ever seen; I watched him in about six or seven plays and he was so brilliant — he could stand with his back to the audience and whisper, and be heard in

the back row of the gallery. John Gielgud, of course, who
was certainly the greatest actor I've seen in my time; I saw
his Hamlet in 1944, and I saw it eighteen times, goggle-
eyed; I've seen 27 Hamlets now and his is still the best.
I suppose in a way it's better that it's not on film because
I wouldn't want the memory of it spoiled.

**The state of the theatre today — it's a very big question,
but what sort of shape are we in?**

I think we've got more good actors than they ever
had; I don't see any of the great actors — Gielgud, Olivier,
Richardson, Wolfit — and I was so fortunate to be around
and learning at the time that they were treading the boards.
In theatre, we've got to be very careful because television
is, in a way, spoiling an audience: on the whole, you don't
laugh at home — you listen to canned laughter and don't
laugh out loud; and laughter is contagious, so if you do laugh
at home you're likely to miss the next line, whereas in the
theatre an actor will put the brakes on and you don't miss
a syllable. But there are wonderful plays being written,
wonderful actors to perform them — as long as there
is a public to watch them.

**You have your knighthood, you have so many glorious
performances behind you — why are you still doing it?**

Because I just love it. I can never understand people who
retire because it means they've never quite enjoyed what
they're doing and they can't wait to get out of it. I've been
an actor for 62 years and I've enjoyed every single minute
of it; I don't want to retire from that — it's too lovely.

Ian Ross

Executive Director, 1998 – 2004

Why did you get into theatre in the first place? What was the attraction?

It was by default, I'm afraid; I can't say there was an attraction in the first instance – that grew on me. I needed to get a job after leaving school and I ended up going to a careers person who offered me one of two things: a trainee theatre technician or a trainee undertaker. To this day, I'd love to know why that person suggested an undertaker, because the words 'solemn' and 'Ian' don't really go together at all.

You've put programmes into so many theatres around the country, but what were your first impressions of turning up at Cambridge Arts Theatre?

My association with Cambridge goes back to before I took over the Arts Theatre because many years ago I worked for Cambridge Theatre Company, who were based above the old Arts Cinema; so my memory of the Arts was always very much a fond one. I thought the auditorium was absolutely magnificent and remembered it very clearly, even though there'd been a long period of time in between; you walk into that auditorium and it grabs you, and I can't personally think of many in the country that are better. It's a really warm and welcoming place, both for the audience and for the actors, and that's borne out by comments from many of the people who've played here in my time – they have all loved the playing relationship between themselves and the audience.

You arrived with a mountain to climb because it was a very troubled inheritance – perhaps you can recall a few of the problems that hit you as you walked through the door?

Well, the Theatre was closed! I arrived, and two weeks later there was no programme, there was nothing and that was a strange one for me, even with all the other problems I've experienced in running a theatre. Setting aside the financial situation, because there was always a way through that, I suppose the thing that really struck me was a lack of confidence – confidence in the Theatre from the public as well as the Theatre having no confidence in itself.

Not only did you have to spearhead a staff who were feeling very demoralised, but you had to choose a digestible programme that suited just about everybody who had ever walked into the Theatre – how do you go about finding that sort of balance in a programme?

What I don't do is programme for what I want; I try to programme for what I think others are looking for. The moment you start programming for yourself and nothing else, it becomes problematic; if I'd programmed for what I wanted all of the time at the Arts Theatre, I could have closed it quite quickly! So I'm interested in the make-up of the community; the Cambridge community is a fascinating one with many different elements – and that's really useful for somebody programming a theatre; they're very knowledgeable and very diverse. I'm interested in putting a programme together which is about embracing as many sectors of the community as possible, and choosing – from what one can afford – the best quality within any given area of the arts. I don't want lowest common denominator stuff – I know I didn't always get that right, but on the whole I think I did.

It's not just a matter of keeping the patrons happy; there's also outside pressure from people who fund theatre activities. Did you ever feel pressurised into putting things on that you actually thought the patrons wouldn't really want to come and see?

Good question and the straight answer is yes; I think every theatre programmer has that experience because you're forever having to balance up the funding organisations who, in turn, have their own criteria to fulfil. Looking back, it would have been nice if the thinking had been a bit more joined

up; what the funders want is not necessarily always thought through in terms of how an organisation can develop that for the future. You have to work with an audience, to take them on a journey, and presenting a piece of work in isolation has its own problems. Now, six years on, people are prepared to take much more of a risk with the programme and book to see things they wouldn't have done before; however, that doesn't mean they're as adventurous as some parties might hope they would be – and it's balancing that which is tricky.

You've brought a number of productions to Cambridge that you must be very proud of: it was a brave and glorious thing to bring the *Ring Cycle* – are you particularly proud of that?

Yes, very. The chairman, Nigel Brown, and I talked about it for a couple of years before actually doing it, and I'm very proud that, in nearly seventy years of the Arts Theatre's history, I was the first person to bring the *Ring Cycle* – who wouldn't be? And it was well received; many people were sceptical about Wagner until they took the plunge and had a go at it, and they were very pleasantly surprised.

What about the other finest hours?

There is one thing that I'm particularly pleased with, and it goes back to the question of how things were when I first arrived. In all the buildings that I've worked in, I can look back and identify a moment that really changed things, a sea-change in attitudes, although I didn't necessarily realise it at the time. The one for me has got to be in my first season, when I programmed a musical from South Africa called *Kat & the Kings*. Everybody looked at it in the brochure and thought I'd lost the plot, but I'd seen it and really believed in the show. When the tickets went on sale, everything else in the season started to sell except that, and we did all sorts of extra left-field marketing but still couldn't shift a ticket. I honestly thought the people of Cambridge would really like the show and that we just had to nudge them a bit, so we gave away lots of tickets for the first night; the vast majority of people who came with free tickets either wrote to me to say how much they'd enjoyed it or sent cheques which were way in excess of what the ticket price was. The box office went absolutely ballistic for the rest of the week and, looking back on it, I think *Kat & the Kings* had a real impact which resonated around the whole community: people were still talking about it four years later. So I'm proudest of that and yes, it's been great to get actors

of the calibre of those in this book to Cambridge – but in terms of changing people's perceptions of the Arts Theatre, *Kat & the Kings* was one of the most important weeks.

You've produced the pantomime for the last five years; that must be one of the biggest tasks in the Arts Theatre's calendar?

It's a huge show for the Theatre. What we embarked upon with Christopher Biggins – and I hope we've achieved it – is to replicate the Cyril Fletcher time. Sometimes it's not necessarily about whether it's Biggins or Cyril Fletcher, though; it's about continuity and familiarity for an audience, about having a traditional pantomime that is done really well – the script is good, the costumes and sets are good, and people can actually sing and dance and act. I'm not a big one for soap stars in panto – you come on and do a ten minute slot, then somebody else comes on and does a ten minute slot, and the story's lost; that's a shame, because the stories are really good. I'm a bit of a sucker for panto.

You must have felt the weight of the Keynes tradition when you first started; is there still room for that kind of personal vision in a regional theatre?

Yes. My God, there has to be. Regional theatre has a real responsibility: it cannot sit on its own and expect everybody to turn up. It has a responsibility to its community, and that's got to have some depth to it – it can't just be a matter of paying lip-service. Theatres often use the word 'education', but they have to acknowledge that it's not just about schoolchildren between the ages of eight and eighteen; it's vital that they embrace a much wider brief, one that goes deeper into the community. If they do that, theatres can help and work with other organisations – health organisations, for example – and can play a really major part in improving people's quality of life. The Arts Theatre genuinely believes in that and realises that its role is about more than just putting on a play, and I hope other theatres are taking that responsibility as well; my impression is that some are and some aren't. In the future, I think those that don't will come across many, many problems; those that do will have a much more rounded existence. Live performance has a lot going for it – it's for the moment, but you're up against a real MTV culture. I didn't realise until the other night that children taking GCSEs now don't have to read a whole Shakespeare; they only have to answer questions on two or three parts, which might be a scene or even just a speech, and that's frightening. That worries me, because how are they going to sit through a whole play if, at the age of fifteen or sixteen, they don't even have to read a whole book? Perhaps I'm being a Luddite about this, but people forget there can be more texture to theatre than 'I recognise that number'.

What would you like your legacy to be?

I'd like to believe that people will work more together in the future. There's a tendency within the arts community *per se*, right across the country, to work in isolation and with a certain amount of fear or envy; I think it would be nice to believe that organisations could work more in partnership, understanding what each can offer the other instead of thinking of the threat. I think what I'm proudest of, though, is the fact that more people want the Arts Theatre now than don't, and when I arrived it was the other way round.

Credits

Nicola Upson *Author*
Nicola Upson read English at Downing College, Cambridge, and graduated in 1991. Since then, she has combined careers in publishing and theatre with work as a freelance writer and critic; her articles and reviews have appeared in magazines and journals on both sides of the Atlantic, including the *New Statesman*, the *Observer* and the *Independent*. She is the author of *Mythologies: the Sculpture of Helaine Blumenfeld* and a contributor to the *Continuum Encyclopedia of British Literature*, and is currently writing a detective novel set in London theatre in the 1930s. She has an eight-year association with Cambridge Arts Theatre, first as Head of Marketing and later as a consultant.

Mandy Morton *Author*
After a successful recording career with Decca and Polydor, Mandy Morton moved into arts journalism and has enjoyed a twenty-year association with the BBC as both a producer and a presenter, specialising in theatre and music biography. Her work for radio includes documentaries on PD James, Clannad, Mary Black, Ray Davies, Michael Crawford, Nana Mouskouri, Richard Briers, Cate Blanchett, Jeremy Irons and Sir Antony Sher, and much of the interview material for this book comes from her extensive archive. She lives in Cambridge, and has supported the work of Cambridge Arts Theatre for more than thirty years.

Julia Hedgecoe *Photographer*
Julia Hedgecoe's career began in Fleet Street, and her photographs appeared regularly in *The Daily Telegraph*, *The Times*, *Woman's Sunday Mirror* and other magazines. She moved to Cambridge in 1989 and concentrated on portrait photography, completing a commission for Churchill College in 1996. In 1998, her portraits of fifty distinguished Cambridge women graduates culminated in a book, *Educating Eve*, and an exhibition at the Arts Theatre which later transferred to the National Portrait Gallery; a number of these photographs are now in the NPG's permanent collection. Her publications include *Treasures of the Embroiderers' Guild*, *The Patchworks of Lucy Boston* and the distinguished visual history of Norwich Cathedral, *Stories in Stone*, photographs from which were used to illustrate two Channel 4 television programmes.

John Carrod *Book Designer*
John Carrod was always likely to be a practitioner of the arts, winning a scholarship at the age of thirteen to a specialist art school in Surrey and going on to train in major London Colleges: Central, Hornsey and the Royal College of Art. During the next ten years he divided his time between being a musician and a designer; achieving little in either he got a 'real job' as creative director of Optimus – a design group in Cambridge. After a spell in the United States he returned to the UK to set up his own design consultancy Carrods with his wife Janet. John now works as a freelance designer and lectures at colleges in the Cambridge area.

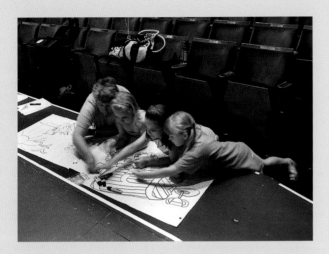

Thank you

In Good Company has been made possible by many
people who have given time, energy and talent, both to
the production of the book and to the creation of a unique
period in the Arts Theatre's history. Grateful thanks go to:

Ian Ross, without whose inspirational programming there
would be no book and who made the Theatre such a very
special place to be; TTPCom Ltd. and Miriam Radford for
their endless support, enthusiasm and patience; Mandy
Morton, for sharing a wealth of glorious material and for
giving more support to the Arts than any theatre could
ever hope for; Julia Hedgecoe and John Carrod for creating
something so beautiful and for being a joy to work with;
Ashley Butten and Piggott Black Bear for so kindly taking
us on; and, most importantly, the performers and the
audiences who keep the whole thing going through
thick and thin.

Nicola Upson